BLACKTHORN
Lore and the art of making
WALKING STICKS

Wanton with long delay the gay spring cometh;
The Blackthorn starreth now his bough
on the eve of May.

Robert Bridges

ACKNOWLEDGEMENT

I wish to acknowledge my indebtedness to the Eaglesham family in Kirkoswald. To Sheena for her constructive criticism of the text and to George for obtaining a supply of Stag horn antlers when all other sources failed. Also to their daughter Gwen, who wrestled with my handwriting and typed the manuscript.

BLACKTHORN
Lore and the art of making
WALKING STICKS

JOHN MURCHIE DOUGLAS

First Published in 1984
by
Alloway Publishing Ltd.,
Ayr.

Reprinted
1985
1988
1995

Printed in Scotland
by
Walker & Connell Ltd.,
Hastings Square, Darvel,
Ayrshire.

Line Drawings by
Ron Davison

ISBN 0 907526 66 7

CONTENTS

PREFACE

Descended from a family which made its living for generations from wood, my earliest memory is of being taken by my father on an expedition to select and mark trees for felling. Brought up in that tradition it is hardly surprising that I have an abiding interest in and fondness for wood and trees.

I considered myself to be reasonably familiar with all our common trees and it was only when I began to delve into the habits of blackthorn, I realised there was a gap in my education. My experience suggests that a great number of people are in the same situation and a fundamental purpose of the book is to share with them, the knowledge I have since acquired.

I may appear over-bold in stating this but I have come to believe that blackthorn is unique and the most complex, interesting and least understood of our wild trees. Furthermore, it is a tree which has been in decline, is relatively scarce and although, as yet, not an endangered species, is often under attack.

Strictly not a botanical treatise, the book is intended for a wide readership; for the generally interested, for the naturalist and for the country craftsman, whose interests are his craft and his raw materials.

It deals first with the natural history of blackthorn, its habitat, environment and manner of growth but in greater width and depth than would normally be found in compendia of trees. In addition, my speculative excursions into folk-lore and other fields present some novel approaches.

Throughout all runs the thread of a kind of detective story describing the step by step process of observation, enquiry and deduction leading to the "final solution" in the closing chapters. These chapters contain the theory and practice of what I believe are original methods of producing blackthorn walking sticks of quality from tree branches which hitherto would have been impossible to use.

Equally as important as its physical attributes, blackthorn possesses another, more elusive, quality which endows a walking stick with character and prestige above all others. The most expressive word for it and closest to a definition is "charisma". In the appropriate chapter, I try, however imperfectly, to provide the reasons.

The chronicle also contains some humorous asides in which I am able to laugh at myself, not always without difficulty, and so lighten the atmosphere.

Most of the material and observations in the text are original and in that respect, I hope it will heighten our appreciation of an unjustly neglected plant.

DON'T BLAME ME!

INTRODUCTION

"A chance in a million" is the only way to describe the circumstance which, some three years ago, led me into a step by step process of observation and discovery and eventually to the writing of this book.

I had been retired and living in the country for a good time and had taken a notion to go fishing again. Not that I was all that keen on the prospect, most of my previous fishing had been in the North of Scotland where a quarter hundred-weight basket of Trout was not uncommon. In contrast, from the rivers and lochs available to me in South Ayrshire, a dozen small fish would be regarded as a good catch. I am not the kind of fisherman who can spend hours on the water, catch nothing and say he has enjoyed his day.

In the event, I was to change course and embark on a pursuit which has given me more pleasure and satisfaction than any fishing I have ever done. It began when checking my equip-ment. I decided I needed a wading stick, and set out to find and cut a suitable ash sapling. On my way out of the wood, walking down through a thicket of blackthorn, I saw a shoot just beside the path, not surprising in a Blackthorn thicket, one might say. The difference was, through the screen of minor branches and leaves, I seemed to see what looked like a straight stem growing out of a right-angled twist at the bottom.

"Cut a stick when you see it" is a sound old country maxim — and I acted on it, stripping of the side branches and expos-ing an impeccable walking stick with straight stem, perfect handle, and of satisfactory weight. Fishing forgotten, I took it home and had trimmed it and fitted a ferrule when realisa-tion dawned and disaster struck, the stick was just too short. There is a correct length for each and every person — a length measured by standing the stick upright on the floor and dropping the arm straight down to meet it. The handle should cut the wrist just above the palm. My stick was a full inch too short for me! One inch might not appear to be much but that amount, plus or minus the relevant length, spoils comfort and proper support. My to be treasured blackthorn stick was flawed.

Beyond an ability to identify blackthorn, and a vague impression that blackthorn walking sticks came from Ireland (a not uncommon belief), I really knew nothing about my subject at that stage. I proceeded, in consequence of my first lucky encounter, in the naive belief that finding another would be a simple matter of searching long enough.

In the following weeks and months, I sought out and explored all the blackthorn thickets and hedges within walking distance of the village. Unsuccessful, I widened the search, by car, to a ten mile radius and further afield – but still without success. By now, I had scanned some thousands of bushes and had found plenty of handles, but on bent or twisted stems and straight stems without handles but the combination of both eluded me. Finding what I was looking for really was "A chance in a million"

My explorations had occupied me more or less throughout the summer, taking me on occasion across pretty rough country and down through steep glens. Gradually an interest in Blackthorn for its own sake had taken over. The variety of shape, size and form and the places where it grows are fascinating, in these respects it is like no other bush or tree. Indeed I feel a tingle of excitement when I set out to explore a new territory not knowing what I am going to find.

In the meantime I turned to the literature and while the many books of trees all provided a paragraph or two and some scattered information on Blackthorn, the details were scanty with nothing at all about walking sticks. Hoping for a specialised book or at least a monograph, I consulted the local library service who kindly undertook a search but reported back that nothing was known. Frustrated, but stubborn, I took up the challenge. If sticks didn't come naturally, I would improve on Nature and find a way of fashioning them. In the end I was reasonably successful, and have produced close to a hundred sticks of various types and contributed to a wood-craft exhibition.

The final step in my personal adventure was that of being persuaded to turn author. My "handiness with blackthorn", as it was put, had spread abroad, and several people had brought me sticks to be straightened. On one occasion, having made due delivery, I had to fend off a persistent questioning as to how I had achieved success. "Look, you are getting on a bit, you know! Don't take your knowledge with you," was the final riposte.

Aware that I have passed my three score years and ten, even if without present intention of going anywhere, I had to admit there was some point to what the man said. And thus, my authorship of the present volume.

THROB! THROB!
IS IT SAFE TO COME OUT?

THE TREE

Prunus spinosa, translating as the Spiny Plum — in English, the Sloe, in Scots, the Slae — that is blackthorn. It is a plum and, more, is the original wild plum which, crossed with the cherry plum, is a parent of our domestic plums, damsons and greengages. Blackthorn is one of our truly native trees, from the beginning of the post-glacial period and with some fossil evidence that it was present in the preceding inter-glacials. A tree of undoubted antiquity.

I am struck particularly by the aptness of the adjective spinosa, which might also be translated as thorny but spiny conveys better, one of the main characteristics of Blackthorn. The thorns appear, in the usual manner of thorns, on the parent branch, thickening at the base and growing then into small branches — but still bearing the thorn at the tip. At a stage of six inches or more of growth the thorn dies away, and the spine, as it should now be called, becomes a branch proper. In this transitional stage from thorn to branch the spine can be deadly. The thorn is hard, and as thin and sharp as a fine hypodermic needle — to an extent that country women once used them as pins for their sewing. When these thorns are attached to a tough, elastic branch able to recoil like a steel spring, it is easy to imagine the damage they can do.

My Latin scholar friend tells me that the suffix "a" in spinosa classifies the plant as a female and in that I concur heartily. If you don't treat them carefully they can scratch like hell and I have the scars to prove it. A momentary lapse of attention to the creature has led me to an operation under general anaesthetic and three nights in hospital! It happened when I pushed my way into the centre of a bush, and a recoiling branch sprang back, driving a thorn into the knuckle bone of my middle finger. I felt the blow, but the thorn was so sharp there was little feeling of jag or pain, and no noticeable bleeding. The embedded thorn remained in my hand for six months before infection boiled over into serious blood poisoning. I have the thorn tip still, in a little glass bottle. It measures 1/16" long, and is as thick as a human hair. The truly cautious stick hunter should wear a thornproof hat, jacket, leggings, goggles and stout leather gloves. Sadly, I seldom practice what I preach.

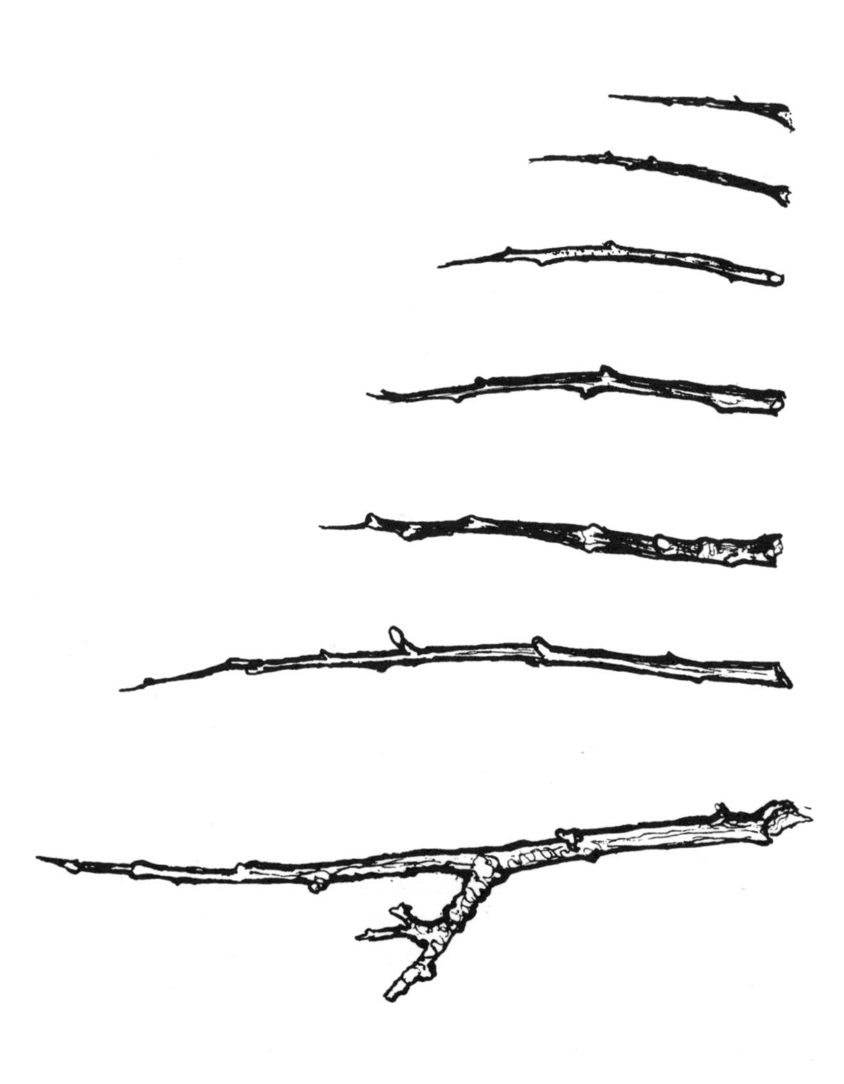

IDENTIFICATION

Most people are familiar with the name blackthorn, associating it mainly with walking-sticks. Sloe is also well known, probably from its use as a flavouring for gin. In contrast, the number who can connect the two is relatively small and those who can identify and pick out a Blackthorn growing, say, in a Hawthorn hedge are fewer still. This is the result of modern living and would not have been true in the past, when the blackthorn touched more closely on the lives of country folk. The fruit was used for making wine and flavouring jam, and old herbalists quote both fruit and bark as specifics for stomach disorders. Morris dancers carried sprigs of the blossom on May Day, although I venture to suggest that the reason was due more to the early flowering of blackthorn and as a substitute for Hawthorn which was regarded as the "magic" tree but bloomed later and was not available on the day. Early water diviners swore by blackthorn twigs as reliable indicators. The branches and cuttings gave a fiercely burning flame and were used for heating ovens. I have already mentioned the use of the thorns as pins in sewing and the leaves were used as a substitute for tea, although, in view of the purgative effect of fruit and bark, I would look on the brew with some suspicion.

In treating the matter of identification, I have avoided the kind of descriptions written by botanists for botanists, favouring instead the following, more practical approach – a short cut, if you like. Blackthorn and hawthorn have a superficial resemblance even from close at hand, and we need concern ourselves only with distinguishing these two wild trees. This, in conjunction with the fact that most, but not all, blackthorn is found alongside or mixed with hawthorn, makes the point that it is enough to be able to distinguish the two species.

In early spring there is no problem. The white blossom of the blackthorn comes out in March or April according to latitude and climate, some weeks before hawthorn. It is the only wild tree with this characteristic and is unmistakeable. During this flowering period I like to tour unknown back roads and mark any new finds for future reference; I have also stood on a commanding hill with binoculars and made some unexpected discoveries.

In summer, identification requires closer examination, and rests on the leaf. That of blackthorn is oval and about 1½ inches long. Hawthorn leaves are lobed, giving them a ragged and quite different look. The experienced eye can sometimes tell the difference at a moderate distance, even when passing in a motor car, but this depends more on a kind of feeling which can be mistaken.

In autumn, too, the leaves can be helpful, even if coloured, but instant recognition is provided by the sloes. These are small, round plums, up to ¾ inch in diameter and growing in bunches. They ripen from green to blue-black in colour with a bloom on the skin. Unfortunately they are not always present, as a late frost can strike the blossom and prevent the setting of the fruit — "a blackthorn winter". Such winters are not uncommon, and neither in 1981 nor 1982 were there any sloes at all in my district.

Identification in winter is extremely difficult, there is no single positive indicator and judgement rests on an accumulation of small pointers — colour, form, bark and thorns. There is no substitute for experience at this time, and experience has been defeated sometimes.

Obviously it is better to find and plot the trees in earlier seasons, and return to known finds in winter, which is the best time to cut a stick. With no sap running and the leaves gone, cutting is easier and the cutter can see what he's doing.

I have, in these last few paragraphs, addressed myself at length to the reader who knows nothing or not much, about blackthorn and who, understandably, might not be fully clear as to the purpose in my comparison with hawthorn. Let me amplify it this way. In most country parishes there are literally hundreds of miles of hawthorn hedges, in contrast blackthorn may be measured in yards. So, if you see an uncut or not recently cut hawthorn hedge, investigate, you might be lucky and find some blackthorn. In short the hawthorn can lead you to it. I will enlarge on this and other related factors in a later chapter. As a cautionary note, I must mention Crab Apple which is also found in hawthorn and due to the dark colour of the branches, can be mistaken for blackthorn. The leaves, although similar in shape however, are larger 2 - 2½ inches long and the Crabs in Autumn provide easy identification. In addition it is generally less thorny, if at all, and the branches are straighter and of more open growth.

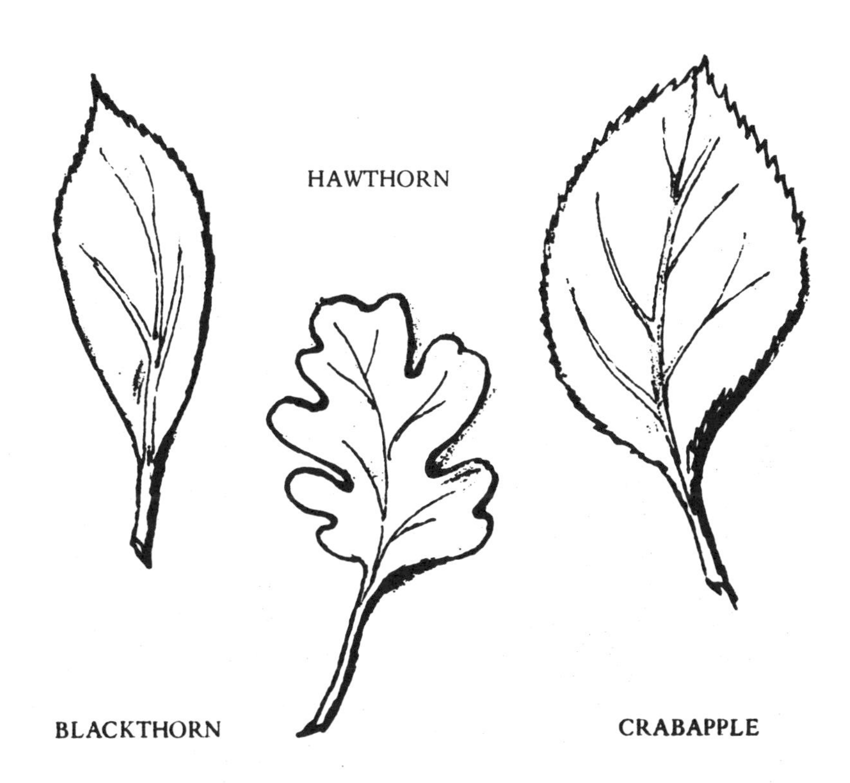

HISTORY, GROWTH AND REPRODUCTION

On the basis of fossil evidence, blackthorn can be presumed to be a genuinely prehistoric tree. While such evidence can give us an indication of its age, it cannot tell its mode and form in that early time. Its unusual and peculiar features, however, lead me to speculate that it is indeed a primitive type which has preserved its original form through the ages, unlike most of our common trees which have adapted to changing conditions by mutation or hybridisation.

Probably the habit of flowering early, before the appearance of leaves, evolved to suit the climate of the period, since nature does nothing without reason. Now, compared with its competitors for living space, such behaviour is a positive disadvantage, (see Blackthorn Winter). Similarly its excessive suckering habit, indicative of adverse conditions in its urge to survive, in this age, has led man to declare war and its replacement by the ubiquitous hawthorn. Furthermore its inordinate spininess, tough wood and dense tangled growth seem to point to a need for defence against predators long extinct.

Historical record testifies to the decline of blackthorn. Archaeological discoveries establish that it was common, and widely used by the early Britons. Hawthorn, in contrast, was not common until the 5th/6th century A.D., when it was adopted by the Saxons for land enclosure. In Scotland and Ireland hawthorn's introduction would have been much later. Since that time, blackthorn's displacement by hawthorn appears to have continued, with the results described in the previous chapter.

Having indulged myself meditating on the past let me return to the present and more easily verifiable facts. Considering now the ways of propagation, there are two. First, seeding, the fruit falls, rots and the tree hopes the seed in the kernel will germinate and grow. With blackthorn the success rate appears to be low — I have come across very few naturally occurring seedlings, and even hand planting of seeds has proved unsuccessful. The consequence is detrimental to the blackthorn in its struggle against hawthorn and other more freely seeding trees. These find their way into its thickets and hedges and threaten dilution and ultimate extinction. If a seedling has been lucky and is growing in open space, untrammelled by other growths, it can reach a height of 16 feet. It takes a tree shape, although the dense crown and tangled branches present an irregular outline. If growing at the edge of a wood, or among other and higher trees, its search for light results in long, scraggy branches.

Suckering is the more successful means of multiplication, and the one on which the tree mainly depends for survival and increase. A 'sucker' is a shoot rising from underground to form a new plant. For clarity I will use the term "ground shoots" to distinguish such suckers from "tree shoots" which grow from the trunk or a branch above ground. There are a number of mysteries in the behaviour of shoots, mysteries for which, I confess, I have no certain explanations.

Blackthorn is a shallow-rooting tree, sending out roots many of which travel outwards only a few inches below ground level, and sometimes attain extraordinary length. Some time ago I had an interesting and informative experience. I came across a blackthorn thicket which had been partially torn out by a mechanical digger, and picked up five roots, intact and still attached to their stems. Four of the roots measured between four and six feet in length, and the fifth one foot. They were all about one inch in diameter at the thickest part.

Who knows what length the roots would have been if left undisturbed? The thicket from which they had come had been formed by suckering and was about eight feet high. On examination, the four long roots owned no suckers, but the short root had two quite respectable shoots. This was strange — five plants, all approximately the same age and size, yet only one had suckered. In seeking an explanation there are three known facts which are linked. (a) It is the instinct of the plant to sucker and multiply. (b) Not all roots sucker. (c) Suckering can occur at any, up to quite a long, distance from the mother plant. Outriders as it were.

Logically, therefore, the assumption must be that a root will sucker only when it finds the right conditions. What these conditions are, soil or others, remains a mystery. Obviously the short root had found an ideal condition close to the mother plant, so much so that it put up two suckers. Having suckered, it put its strength into the shoots and starved its own growth. In brief the root had not suckered because it was short, it was short because it had already suckered. The long shoots had not yet found what they were seeking.

To summarise, it might be said that the mother plant sends out roots as probes, and when an ideal spot is found, it puts up a shoot. I have dwelt on their factors at some length, since they help as to understand the great variations in sucker and thicket growth.

THICKETS

I want to take you now to a thicket, the progress of which I have monitored for three years. I have watched it expand and fan out to cover an area of ground about twenty five yards wide by fifty yards long. The small group of mature trees which spawned it occupies only a tiny corner of the site. The child has outgrown the parents a hundred fold.

Situated on a rough and uneven piece of land, sloping down from an unfenced road to a burn, it has filled the width between and so continued to march and extend its fifty yard length. The thicket is now self-sustaining and prolific – its progress is unrestricted, and it has no further need of an umbilical cord to its parents, who have created a rampant monster. The growth is dense and absolutely impenetrable, the shoots so close together that a rabbit could scarcely find a way through. It is a startling thought that, the estimated area of about 1250 square yards could contain anything up to 10,000 shoots.

The ground is waste – unlikely ever to have been cultivated or even grazed – and must certainly be infertile. Willow-herb or fireweed likes these conditions, and flourished here until overtaken and destroyed by the remorseless blackthorn.

Blackthorn seems endowed with the ability to regulate the height of its thickets. Generally the height of trees increases with age, and in a thicket which has taken some years to develop, one would expect the younger shoots to be progressively shorter than the older ones, giving a close-knit example, like mine, the appearance of a sloping roof. In fact, however, the young shoots quickly catch up and keep the whole thicket at a fairly uniform height – in this case about six feet at this time. Viewed from a distance it appears rather like a rolling tide. A little reflection suggests an underlying direction and purpose – the new shoots being the spearhead of the advance must be strong and vigorous. Those in the rear only consolidate territory already won. The whole thicket gives and impression of planned advance – when it meets an obstacle, or condition it finds inimical, such as the flooding area of a burn, it doesn't waste time but changes direction and pours its energies into any way still open.

It would be a fascinating exercise, if a little difficult without a commandeered fire-engine, to wash away the soil to expose the total root system of a thicket like this. It is, however, possible to deduce with reasonable accuracy the formation, from the regular and close spacing of the shoots and their distance from the parent trees. Simply, the mother tree sent out a root which quickly formed a sucker to become a shoot; the shoot, in its turn, sent out its own roots which put up more sucker shoots, and so on. In fact the thicket is one tree with one root and up to 10,000 branches – or more accurately a number of trees corresponding to the small number of parent trees. If one could uncover the whole root area, it would probably look like a tangled wide-meshed net. Who can say, after all that, that trees cannot think? Primitive peoples believed spirits resided in trees and their elementary thinking, applied to facts such as those revealed above, make their belief easy to understand.

Finished here, we travel by winding back country roads for about three miles to see the extreme of contrast in another thicket, which as far as my knowledge goes is unique. It is situated in what once was an old country garden – the evidence lies in the scattered stones from the cottage walls and in the jet-black soil – jet black from the soot dumped there out of a belief that it was good for the soil, or because the housewife found the garden a convenient place to rid herself of chimney sweepings. In any case the top soil is deep and friable, containing very little clay, and rather like fine sand in texture. The thicket had originated in a high blackthorn hedge growing by the roadside. It is about half the size of the first thicket and has more or less ceased to expand. It is certainly older, and about four feet taller, and the stems of the shoots are thicker.

The strange and perplexing contrast exists between the impenetrability of the first thicket, with its shoots only

BLACKTHORN IN SNOW

Shoots coming up 12 feet from parent trees.

Shoots coming up 20 feet from parent trees.

inches apart, and the widely spaced shoots of this second find. Here I could walk through freely, from end to end. Viewed from outside, the thicket looks like a small pillared hall, the crown of branches forming the roof and the tree stems the pillars. Apart from its size, the first thicket is typical of many, but nowhere had I ever seen anything like the second. I cannot even offer a guess for the unusual configuration, beyond the too plausible and simple reference to soil type and condition.

Some trees, particularly large and mature examples, do not sucker, and this is true of some smaller plants in hedges or established thickets. Others sucker in moderation and can throw up shoots a good distance away from the parent, but without developing into thickets. On the whole, however, it a census were to be taken, we should find that the majority of plants will sucker in some degree. The differences of degree will find an explanation in the soil, the weather and other factors — but the timing and placing of the suckering habit remains a profound mystery.

WHERE IT GROWS

In this account of the places where blackthorn can be found, I cannot claim any knowledge beyond that accumulated in prospecting my own district. Fortuitously however, it is so varied in character that it is hard to imagine a setting in any other part of the country which does not have its prototype here. It behoves me then to acquaint the reader with its placement and geography and my connection with it.

The territory is the northern part of Carrick, a one time province of Galloway and now part of Ayrshire. It stretches from Ayr in the north almost to Girvan in the south and eastwards from the sea to Loch Doon. It is my native country and after many years away I returned to retirement on the outskirts of Kirkoswald, a small village two miles from the sea, and four miles south of Maybole, ancient capital of Carrick.

The scene varies from rocky coast to hills and high moors, with rich farmland between. There is an abundance of wood-land and numerous water courses and small glens. The interior has a maze of narrow roads, and, needless to say, hedges galore. I know of nowhere with so much diversity of country within such narrow bounds – usefully, the furthest points can be reached within a ten mile journey from my base.

Before the mid-eighteenth century, this part of Scotland was wild and largely uncultivated, with little woodland. In these conditions it can be assumed that blackthorn flourished. By 1800, all had changed. The land had been divided into fields enclosed by hedges, and brought into cultivation which included the extensive planting of trees. The programme of improvements must have decimated the blackthorn, with only the glens and wild places left to the survivors.

We have no record of what plant was used for hedges but due to the readiness with which it can be grown from seeds or cuttings it is most likely to have been hawthorn. It is also, a

Contrasting hedges of similar height.

Dense branches

Open branches

Open hedge with widely spaced shoots

Amost tree-height bush in mixed hedge.

Close-up view

Stand of full-height tall trees in farm garden.

long-living plant – some of the hedges we see today could well have been planted 200 years ago. The other possibility is mixed planting, it is a local tradition and within living memory farmers were still mingling hawthorn, blackthorn and crab apple. The practice, at whatever time it was introduced, must have given a new lease of life to the blackthorn, and is certainly responsible for the scattered remnants still found today in hawthorn hedges.

I am doubtful whether any traces of the original stock still survive. I have seen so much dead and dying blackthorn that my impression is that it is not a long-living species. Taking account of its migratory habit, most apparently wild growth can easily be traced back to a man planted hedge or at least to where a hedge probably had been. For example, I know two glens only a field's width apart, each with a burn. One has blackthorn right to the water's edge, the other has none. The difference is that the first glen has been colonised by a hedge growing along the edge of the field at the top.

I have plotted forty-six sites all told. Considering that the area involved must be around one hundred and fifty square miles and even if as I must, have missed a few sites, the ratio emphasises the scarcity of Blackthorn. It is only a fraction of what its population must have been. In my count I have included only stands of six plants or more. The total can be apportioned as follows: Glens 6, Others 12, Roads 28. "Others" include seaward facing coastal slopes and cliffs, field hedges, open spaces and old railway lines.

Coastal slopes can be prolific, and if any of the old wild stock does survive I would judge it most likely to be here. The field hedges are interior hedges, as distinct from march or perimeter hedges, and those containing blackthorn are rare. Open spaces contain the only free standing groves of mature trees. Blackthorn was planted on railway lines to prevent trespassing.

Roads or properly road sides, by virtue of their frequency and ease of access but also in variety offer the best prospects but the accent must be on age. The verges of new or improved roads are generally useless, as blackthorn planting stopped not long after 1900, and one must therefore look for roads built before then and unaltered since. This involves going into the "back country" and along narrow roads, little more than cart tracks. On foot, this is one of the outstanding pleasures of the pursuit. A walk with a purpose, a tangible goal, at the end is vastly superior to an aimless stroll or just walking the dog.

Where a new road has been formed by eliminating the bends from an old one, and where the bends have been left as lay-bys, blackthorn can often be found in the bordering hedge. Where a new road has been given a new direction, the route of the old road can be traced and will often merit close inspection. Historians and others can trace old roads and boundaries by this means. North of Kirkoswald, and parallel to the trunk road, a line of blackthorn indicates (in the middle of a field) the line of the original road.

The type of growth one might normally expect to find in hedges is bush-like. The bushes will have suckered at some time and will have a number of roots and stems — a small thicket in fact. Less often it will have an open growth with a smaller number of stems. Where a hedge has encroached on the road and been cut, the plants will have formed a mass of small, impenetrable branches, and the only way to get into it is from the back. Depending on age and whether the hedge has been cut, its height can range up to tree height, although that is unusual. Blackthorn is a slow growing tree, but the variations in height I find rather perplexing — a hedge on site for 200 years has reached barely ten feet. Does a process of successive periods of dying down and regeneration take place? It would require more than a human lifetime of observation to elucidate all the habits and behaviour patterns of the blackthorn.

Turning again to old roads, with side verges presumably intended to facilitate the passing of carts and useful now when two cars meet, we find blackthorn taking possession of the ground to an extent which threatens to reach the road. My cottage sits on an old road of this style which, a quarter of a mile further on, has become disused. The blackthorn on either side has closed in, met in the centre, and closed the road completely. Blackthorn hedges separating cultivated fields from waste ground, finding their development thwarted on one side by the farmer's activities, form thickets on the other side.

I have indicated that while blackthorn is found in road-side, perimeter hedges, it is rare in hedges dividing fields, and it is interesting to wonder why this should be so. From the winding and sharp changes in direction, obviously the roads were laid down originally to serve scattered farms. They must have been made about the time of the enclosures, when new farms were being created and the roads would, in part, form natural boundaries. The first concern of the farmers would have been to fortify their entire holdings, and only later would they have given attention to internal field hedges. The differences in time of planting, and purpose of the hedging, might explain the differing nature of the hedges, traces of which still remain. Similarly, with stands found in glens and on banks of steep-sided burns, their frequency of occurrence could be due to blackthorn's usefulness as a cattle-excluder.

Old road built over 200 years ago by the then Earl of Cassillis, as a short-cut from Culzean to the new Adam designed church at Kirkoswald The road now closed by blackthorn can be seen on the horizon.
This is the road on which further down my cottage sits.

Line of disused railway. In distance passing under south exit road from Dunure.
View from A719.
Mostly hawthorn but with blackthorn in places.

Line of old road with blackthorn mixed with other trees.
Taken from new trunk road.

Old road with mixed blackthorn and hawthorn hedges.

Blackthorn growing on buttress of dismantled old railway bridge.

Close-up view.

BRANCHES

I have now almost completed the natural history of my subject — the "Lore" as I have called it — and am about to start writing on the art and craft of making walking sticks. Some readers will have been waiting, no doubt impatiently if they resisted reading the last chapters first, for this development. I have used the word "art" advisedly, as we are dealing with the ways of choosing and working a natural growth with the objective of enhancing its appearance and tailoring it for practical use.

The type and growth of the branch is fundamentally important because, while we can alter the shape, we cannot change the basic form which passes on its special character to the stick. You can cut a coat, but you cannot change the pattern of the cloth — there are sticks and sticks! Colour matters too — all blackthorn is not black! In this chapter I intend to link the world of nature to the world of the craftsman.

I look at different branches from the point of view of their suitability — their advantages and disadvantages, the superiority of one over another — for walking sticks. I must confess the subjectivity of my opinions, my partiality to particular types of branch. There are four kinds, although there can be quite wide variations in growth within each. I classify them as tree branches, tree shoots, ground shoots and seedlings.

Tree Branches

Tree branches grow from the stem of the tree, or from their larger branches, in a manner which produces the dense tangled growth typical of blackthorn. Their length and thickness depend on age and their position on the tree or bush. They are spiny and later become covered with small side branches. The abrupt changes in direction of growth that can occur form angles suitable for the fashioning of handles. The

NEW BREEKS
!

colour varies from dark brown to black; the older the branch the darker, generally, is the colour.

Tree branches provide the best walking sticks, the stubs of the side branches being left on to give the prized knotty, knobbly appearance which, together with the colour go to make up the ideal blackthorn stick – a great rarity. The one unvarying characteristic of blackthorn is its perversity, which makes it virtually impossible to find a branch without a bend, or fork, or angle (or all three!) somewhere in its length. Without an effective method of straightening and removing the kinks, the branch is useless.

I am aware that this view is not universally accepted, and must qualify it to some extent. The habit of carrying a stick is still common in the country, and I have seen many blackthorns with rudimentary handles (or none at all), bent and gnarled as when cut from the tree, to which sticks the owners are greatly attached. There is a certain attraction about these and I would admit that a "ruler-straight" stick lacks character. I have a blackthorn which, but for its colour, could be mistaken for an ash plant of the kind able to be produced in hundreds. I am not, therefore, opposed to leaving moderate bends and bumps – but they must be symmetrical to the central axis. I could go even further, and confess that I always look for unusual growth features which might lend distinction to the stick.

Exceptional to the general rule, some branches found in a light-shaded location can be long and much straighter, having more of the qualities of a shoot. Another variety seems more like a cross between a branch and shoot, with some of the attributes of each, illustrating again the many sided-ness of blackthorn. This one sprouts, usually from a thicker branch, at approximately right-angles, and grows faster and longer than its neighbouring branches, if not quite to the extent of a shoot proper. It will have side branches, and can be dark in colour. By using the base branch to carve a handle it can make quite a good stick, provided the stem is straightened.

TYPICAL ROUGH BRANCHES BEFORE STRAIGHTENING

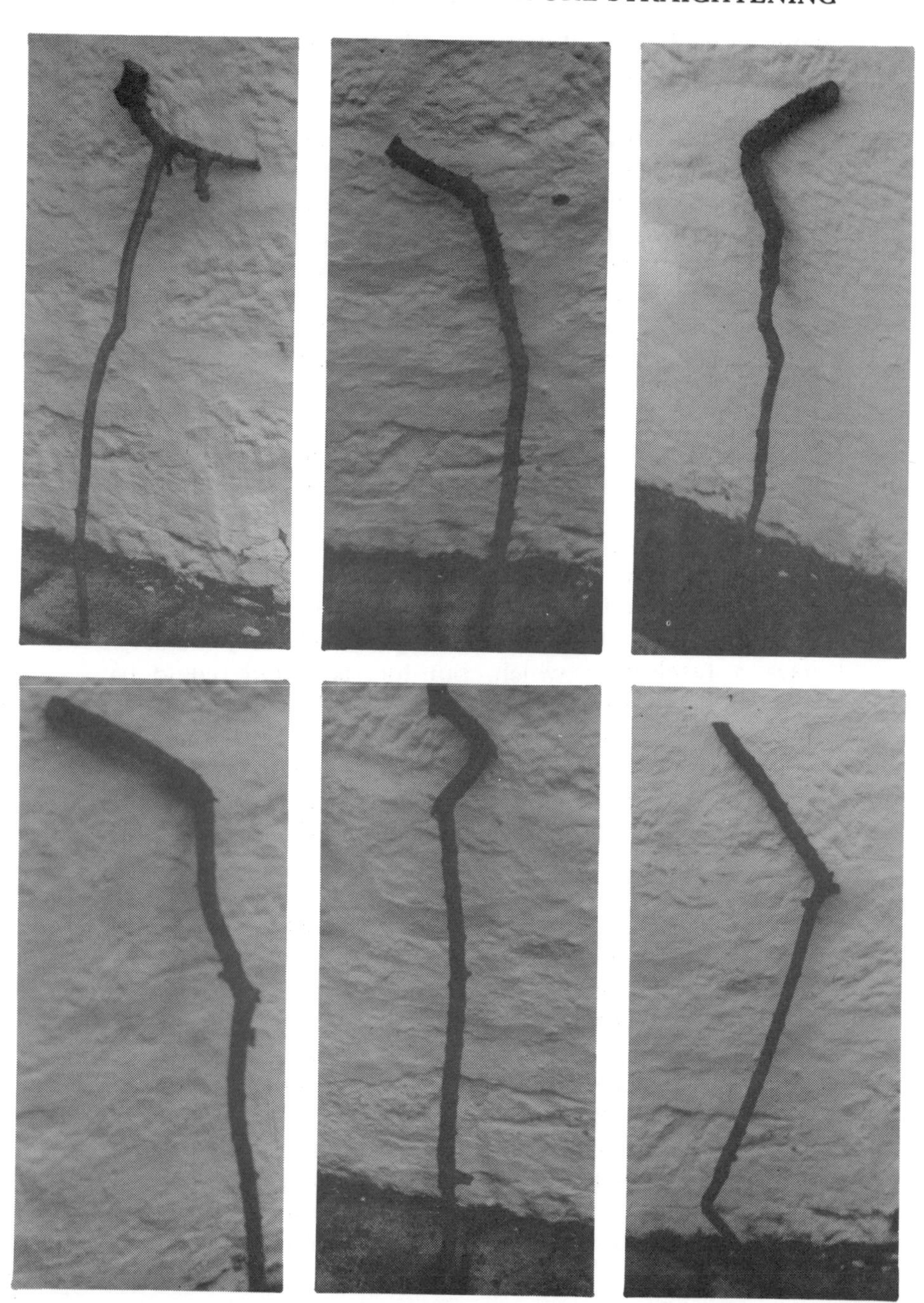

TYPICAL ROUGH BRANCHES BEFORE STRAIGHTENING

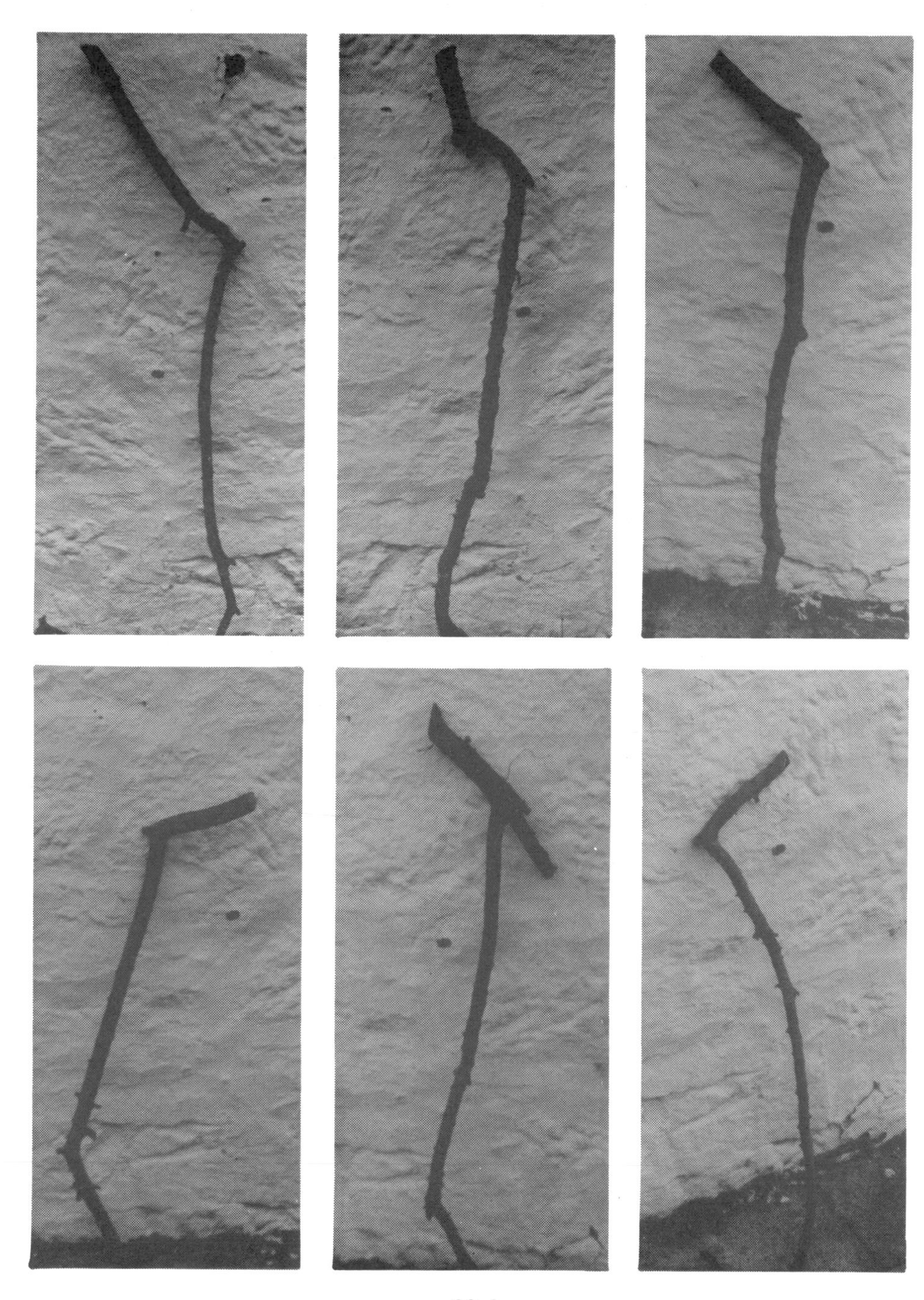

I come now to a variation which is indeed rare, to an extent that in all my travels I have seen no more than four or five. It is so rare that I feel its fully justifies the description of a "sport". It grows in the shape of a flattened "S" and the bark has a unique dimpled appearance. I am unable to decide whether it is branch or shoot, and I first saw it in a walking stick inherited from my grandfather. My second sighting gave rise to an amusing little ancedote. It was late autumn and I was returning from a visit to an outlying village. I had taken a detour to have a look at some blackthorn I had found in summer and wanted to see with the leaf off. I parked my car and walked up the line of bushes, growing at the roadside on a steep bank and behind a fairly deep ditch, until I saw this branch growing parallel to the stem of its bush and almost hidden behind it. I could just see part but that was enough to make me determined to have it.

There was no way of reaching it without going into the ditch and, pressed slacks and polished shoes and all, I slid into about eight inches of water on top of two inches of mud. The branch was a perfect specimen of its type, and required little alteration — the finished stick has a wavy, snake-like shape and is in truth a rare curiosity. There is a moral to the tale however. A short time later I passed that way again and found the roadmen had been at work — all they had left were the stumps of the bushes.

Tree Shoots

Tree shoots are branches run wild, and are well named. They can appear on any part of the tree or bush, at any height, and their speed of growth outstrips many times the growth of normal branches. The direction of growth is upwards, sometimes straight, sometimes twisting and turning, and stretching on occasion as high as the parent plant. The diameter increases with age but remains fairly regular from top to bottom. I have seen old shoots, growing from low down on the tree, which reached twelve feet in height and had a diameter of two inches. As straight as a clothes pole, indeed,

HE SAID THERE WAS A BONE DOWN HERE!

they would have made good clothes poles. Others almost as long, have had a diameter of only one inch.

In contrast, I have seen a shoot put forth, from a fork in a branch near tree top height. The shoot itself was still short – about five feet – and growing at an angle of 45° to the tree.

Generally the stems remain smooth, and the production of side branches is delayed until the shoots have reached a fair height. At that height, side branches develop near the tip. In the twisted variety, the twists occasionally take the shape of handles, and I possess a stick obtained in this way, with a perfect handle and shank (after straightening). It fails to measure up to exacting standards, however, in two respects – its colour is very light brown, and the smoothness of its shank, which results from an absence of side growths on the parent shoot. It would not be readily recognised as blackthorn. If I had to classify sticks from tree shoots I would have to award them a "3rd" grading.

Ground Shoots

The reader will be familiar with the nature and habits of growth of ground shoots from earlier chapters on Growth and Thickets. Undoubtedly they are the most abundant source of raw material for walking sticks, and I suggest that most stick-makers would look no further. Two elements contribute to this circumstance. Compared with branches, ground shoots are relatively straight, and from the shallow growth it is possible to find roots running at right angles to the stems, which can make handles. Let me put it this way – if you are prepared to do enough digging to find a suitable root, and if luck allows the root to coincide with a straight enough stem, you have a useful stick. Its place on the scale of quality is another matter.

If, however, you have the skill to straighten stems and bend handles it reduces dramatically the uncertainty of chance, and effectively increases many times the number of shoots

WHAT'S HE AFTER, RABBITS?

from which not just sticks, but quality sticks can be produced.

A minor disadvantage springs from a fact of plant-life – the shoot normally only begins to grow side branches some distance from the ground, so the "knobbliness" is confined to the lower part of the stick, or is absent altogether. Also, depending on the age of the shoot, the wood can be sappy, leading to wrinkling of the bark when seasoning takes place. On the credit side the handles from the root-handles can take, or be made to take pleasing shapes. I have fashioned a goodly number of attractive sticks from ground shoots, but my first preference is still for those made from branches.

Seedlings

Seedlings generally grow straight stems with many side branches from near ground level, and to this extent should make excellent stick shanks. Unfortunately they seldom have any growth suitable for handles. I refer to this in a succeeding chapter on handles.

I have tried to outline the main variations of branches and shoots. It should be understood, however, that within each variation occur many lesser variables which are easier seen than spoken about. Indeed it is these small differences which help to maintain a lasting interest in Blackthorn.

How to cut a stick

It would be wrong to leave the subject without saying something about how to cut a stick. Blackthorn branches and shoots do not grow in places to suit your convenience, and some are literally unreachable without the proper tools. In the case of one at the top of a high tree, I suppose a solution might be to cut the tree down, but I must express reservations on that course of action. In less drastic, more frequent, circumstances, branches are found at arm's length inside

A

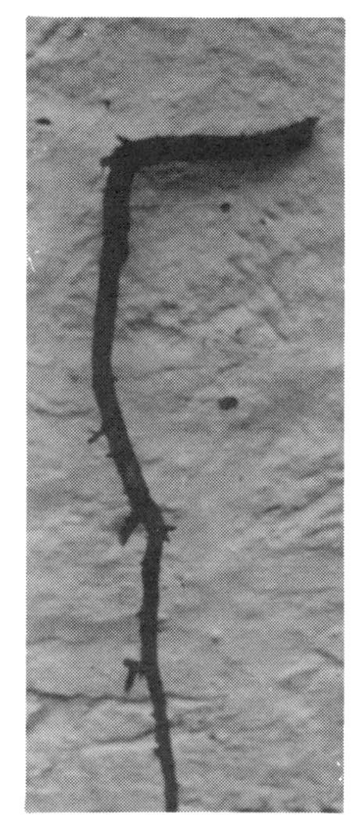

C

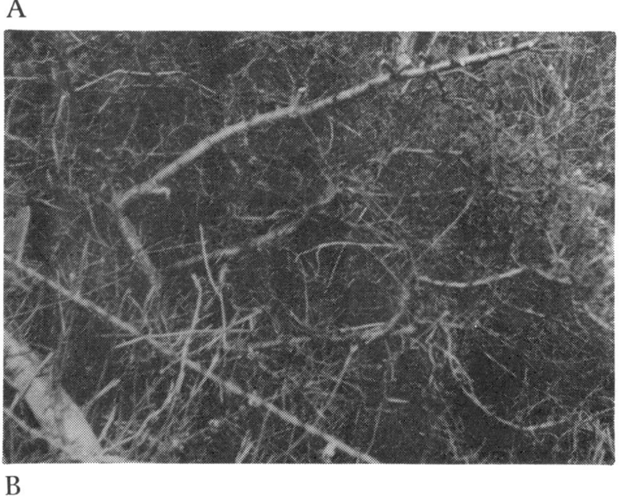

B

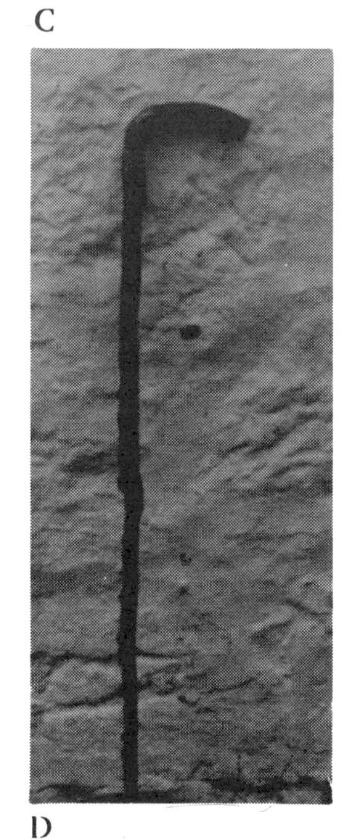

D

A STICK IN HEDGE

B STICK EXPOSED

C STICK CUT

D FINISHED WALKING STICK

hedges. Secateurs are essential to snip away small branches to allow entry, the whole operation is often one handed. Also necessary is a saw with a narrow blade — ideal is my folding pruning saw, which I can slip into a trouser pocket. Opened, it is eighteen inches long, and effectively extends my arm length to about forty inches.

If the sought after branch is further away than that, either you cut a bigger hole in the hedge to squeeze into, or you give up. Assuming that you have managed to cut the branch, a walking stick with a curved handle is needed to pull the branch to a position where it can be gripped. I can assure the reader that, having carried out the operation on many occasions, the advice is offered quite unfacetiously.

Access to shoots is usually easier, but you require a trowel to expose the roots before using the saw. In the light of this my previous comment about leather gloves etc. will be appreciated.

FOOTNOTE:— It is perhaps useful to define the terms I habitually use. The "stick" is the complete walking stick, including the handle; the "stem" is the branch or shoot before straightening — after this treatment it becomes the "shank".

COLOUR

This chapter will be short, but very relevant. The colour of the bark is an essential complement to the other factors which have established the superiority of blackthorn over all other woods from which sticks are made. The practice of peeling the bark from a blackthorn stick, which is sometimes done, destroys its uniqueness and special character.

Like all matters blackthorn, the cause of the colour variations in branches and shoots is obscure. It would be too easy to dismiss it by saying that the colour darkens with age for, while this tends to be true, it is not the whole story. Older branches can be brown, while others, younger, can be jet black or almost so. And why, in a thicket, are the branches on one side of a path of a different shade to those on the other side? All originate from the same source, and grow in the same soil.

The explanation may lie partly in the presence of a fine moss which flourishes in the moist climate of western Scotland. It seems to grow on some plants and not others, and imparts a grey-brown appearance to the bark. The outer bark of blackthorn is extremely thin, and the tiny moss-roots may bleach the colour. No other harm is caused, and the moss can be removed by scrubbing with a stiff-bristle brush and water. On no account must a wire brush or sandpaper be used.

I put forward moss penetration as an hypothesis only, with the further reservation that, even if I am correct, it does not explain all the variations. Every facet of blackthorn seems to contain a mystery. Lest I be accused of carrying my purism to excess, I hasten to say that while a jet black stick remains the ideal, the dark brown colour is perfectly acceptable.

Colour must have been important, also, to the old stick makers. I have heard of one who, long ago, painted or black-varnished his finished sticks. More recently I saw two black-thorn sticks in a retail shop obviously made from shoots, which had been painted or stained all over. I also noticed not long afterwards that they had been sold. The practice of darkening ash or hazel sticks is also not unknown. Two cases are not much to go on, but they are enough to make me wonder if there is a tradition of staining blackthorn — whatever the case, the significance of colour is stressed by the practice.

A brief digression is necessary into the composition of tree bark — . Bark is composed of three layers, the inner bark, the outer bark and between them what botanists call the bark cambium, this produces the cells forming the outer bark. In blackthorn and bear in mind, we are concerned only with wood of the diameter required for handles, about one inch, the over-all thickness of the bark is approximately one sixteenth of an inch.

The outer bark i.e. the black or dark layer is about the thickness of stiff paper, the bark cambium is only of microscopic proportion and the inner bark constituting the greater part, makes up the remainder. Without benefit of a microscope I found it impossible to isolate the cambium layer, but if the outer bark is peeled off its inner surface shows a red colouration which I deduce is the cambium. The red colour is not discernible in all bark, but becomes stronger as the diameter of the branch increases. Slight though it may be, it can affect the colour of the finished handle.

It happens in this way. Practically all handles have to be streamlined, as it were, using a woodrasp and sandpaper to remove high points and projections and to modify bends. During this process the colours of the various layers of bark and sapwood are exposed — successively, from the outside, black, red, brown and light brown. These colours, and the shadings between, create a very attractive wood finish, an effect similar to that found in a piece of fine antique furniture.

It really is essential to varnish the stick and handle. Before this finishing process, the wood appears lifeless and dull, but on the first application of a clear varnish the colours come alive in a quite miraculous way. Irish stick-makers used, and may still use, repeated rubbings of butter to achieve the same effect.

All of the above advice refers to handles made from branch bends. Handles from the roots of shoots can be treated in the same way with equally pleasing results and can make up for the shortcomings of their shanks. Handles carved from thick branches necessarily have had most of the bark removed, and are not in the same class.

A WALKING STICK AND A PIECE OF STRING

When the first Homo Sapiens, or perhaps our even remoter ancestor, the ape-like Homo Erectus, picked up a broken branch and found that it extended his reach and strengthened his arm, man had discovered the stick.

Anthropologists are in disarray about the date of origin of mankind, but the compass of time would certainly be measured in millions rather than thousands of years. Within that scale the exact time when the stick became man's oldest artefact is unimportant. It has certainly been with us for a great enough time to have become embedded in our genes, part of our race memory.

The list of its uses is endless – as an aid to disability, as a tool at work, as a shepherd's crook, as a farmer's "Stick and piece of string", and as measuring rod. In other forms, the stick has been stave, thumb-stick and ski-stick (which might be seen as a specialised kind of walking-stick).

Apart from the purely utilitarian, there are other aspects of sticks which more convincingly illustrate man's subconscious bond to the stick. It is used as a badge of office and mark of rank, and finds a place in traditional and ceremonial occasions. It can become an object of art and collector's piece; history and literature are full of allusions.

The sceptre of Royalty, as a symbol of authority, traces its origins back at least as far as ancient Egypt, and is no more than a stylised stick. The rulers of many primitive peoples carried special sticks indicative of chieftainship. The fasces – the insignia of a Roman magistrate – was a tied bundle of sticks, and Roman centurions carried sticks of olive-wood. It seems unneccessary to mention that Moses carried one.

The sword can be seen as a development of the fighting stick, made possible by the availability of worked metal, and when the practice of carrying swords was discontinued officers adopted the walking stick as a sword-substitute. Similarly in

A

B

C

TREE BRANCHES (SHOOT TYPE)

A – AS SEEN IN BUSH.

B – WITH SIDE BRANCHES REMOVED.

C – AS CUT FOR STICK.

SPRING

SUMMER

WINTER

BLACKTHORN
IN AUTUMN

Jock making
suggestions to
Kirsty.

FIELD
HEDGE

IMPENETRABLE
THICKET

GROUND SHOOTS

BRANCHES

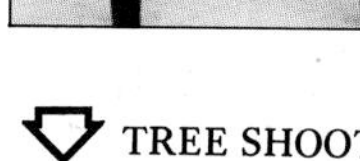

TREE SHOOTS

BRANCHES

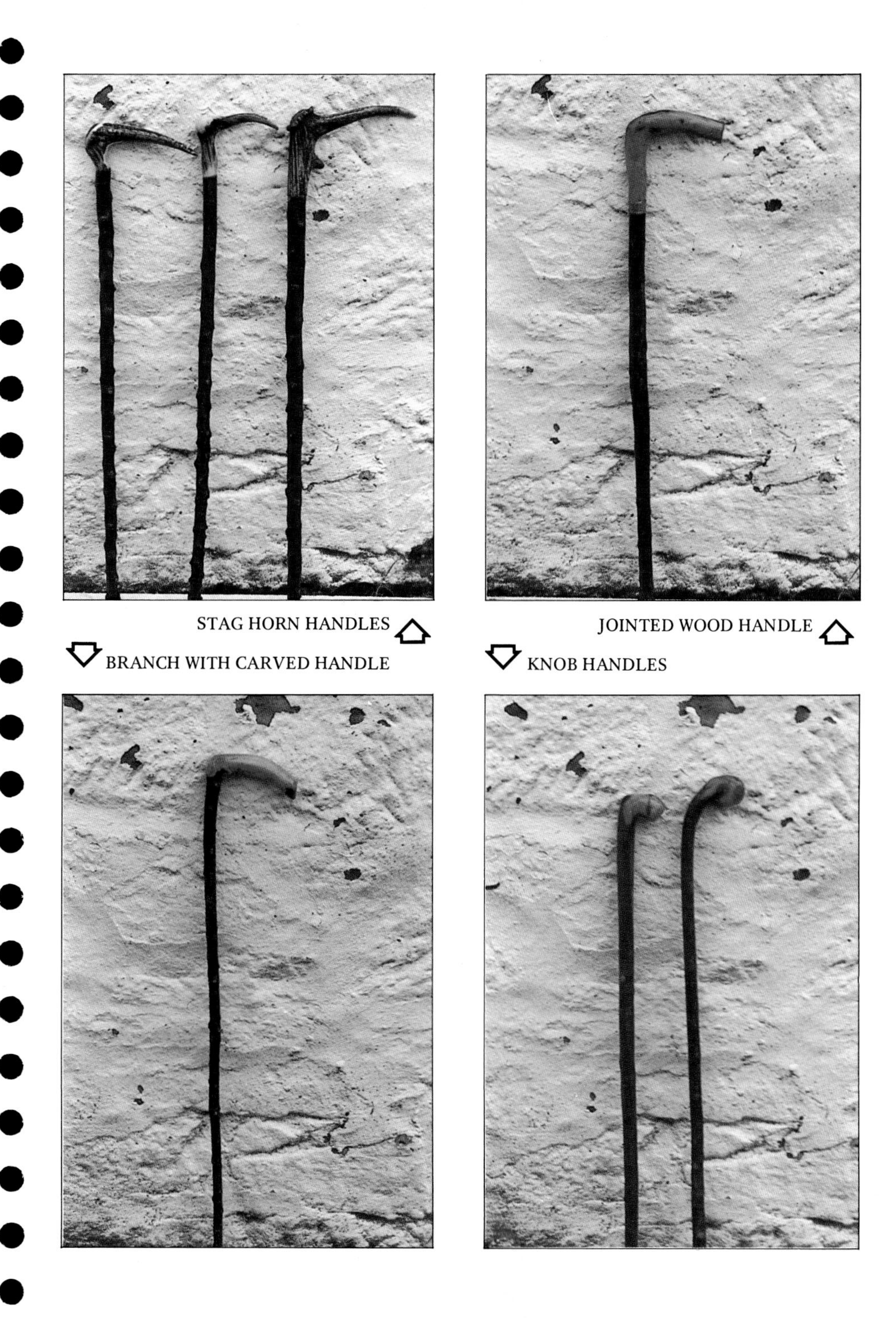

STAG HORN HANDLES

JOINTED WOOD HANDLE

BRANCH WITH CARVED HANDLE

KNOB HANDLES

BLACKTHORN HEDGE ON LEFT SHOWS LINE OF OLD ROAD.

NEW ROAD ON RIGHT.

CROSSRAGUEL ABBEY IN BACKGROUND.

SCRAGGY OLD TREES WITH KIRSTY, JOCK AND TESSA, AND PENNY IN BACKGROUND.

BLACKTHORN TREES IN BLOOM SHOWS PRESUMED LINE OF OLD ROAD CUTTING THROUGH FIELD.

EXPANDING THICKET

STUNTED MOSS COVERED BUSH
Handle of Stick formed from join. (in circle)

CONTRASTING GROWTHS

BLACKTHORN HEDGE BORDERING OLD ROAD. ONE TIME ONLY WAY IN OR OUT OF KIRKOSWALD. BEFORE THE MAYBOLE TO GIRVAN ROAD WAS BUILT.

BLACKTHORN IN BLOSSOM

OLD CARRIAGE ROAD FROM CULZEAN TO KIRKOSWALD COMPLETELY CLOSED BY ENCROACHING BLACKTHORN ON BOTH SIDES.

Court circles, when the sword was outlawed courtiers and gentlemen took to carrying ornate and costly sticks. That tradition was continued in the silver topped cane which complemented top-hat and opera cloak. That a walking stick has a pull to man deeper than as just prop and help on a steep hill, seems also borne out by those many people who, having no material need, automatically reach for a stick, and who in its absence have a sense of something missing. The motor car has unfortunately largely stifled this instinct — perhaps because it has almost killed the habit of walking! It is a futile but entertaining speculation to wonder how our world and we would have developed if nature had designed trees to grow without branches, and man had never seen a stick.

Leaving the abstract for more concrete facts, almost every material available has been used for walking sticks; ranging through precious metals, ivory, ebony, horn, rare woods and others. Of necessity the exotic materials and costly embellishment are confined to the handle, the sheer length of the shank limiting it to more conventional materials (although sometimes even this is ornamented by carving.) In consequence, handle and shank are made separately and then joined together in some way.

For the more common-place sticks the woods selected are those which can be bent easily to form handles, woods like cane, ash, hazel and alder. Although blackthorn does not fall into this category, where bends or curves are present on a branch or root they can be formed into proper handles by a method similar to that for straightening branches and shoots outlined in the next chapter.

Large numbers of straightenable branches and shoots would thus seem to hold little prospect of forming proper handles integral with the shank. These can however be utilised in a number of ways — the simplest being to leave attached a thicker piece of root or parent branch when first cutting, and use it to fashion a knob handle. While it carries the cachet of Blackthorn, and while the great majority of Blackthorn sticks are of this type (including those made commercially), yet on my own scale of values such a stick is of inferior grade and has little appeal.

At the opposite end of the prestige scale would be the blackthorn shank with handle from the point of a stag antler – valuable, too, in the financial sense, yet, ironically, the easiest to manufacture. Shank and handle can be joined by whittling a peg on the shank to fit a hole drilled up the stem of the antler – the skill lies in aligning hole and peg concentrically. A plastic filler makes an effective fixative. The snag is that any antlers are hard to get, and those with well-shaped points are harder still. I always feel saddened to find a staghorn handle wasted, to my way of thinking, on a hazel or ash shank. Similar techniques can be employed with a ram's horn, although here skill is required in shaping the handle, and in fitting a band at the join of handle and shank, a precaution not required with stag's horn. Other than trimming off excess material stag-horn cannot be manipulated, and must be used as it comes.

While the use of other materials is possible, the only remaining practical choice is the carved wood handle. In this district at least, the practice is traditional and fairly common, although mostly on hazel shanks. The shapes vary according to the fancy of the craftsman, and the method of fixing is as described above (on thinner shanks, a steel rod may be used as a peg). Wooden handles can be taken from a solid block of timber, and many are, but it is then impossible to avoid a cross grain at some part of the curve, which can be a weakness. A safer method is to use a thick branch with a curve or bend, which can be followed to give an almost straight grain. When I come across a likely specimen I cut and store it for possible future use.

Both handle and shank offer scope for the wood carver, and I have seen a great diversity of shapes. I suppose a miniature horse's hoof and fetlock would appeal to a horseman, as would a fish shape to an angler. On the shank, among other fancies, horizontal rings are sometimes cut, and recently I saw a shallow circular groove simulating the mark of ivy growing up the stem. I have, in fact, a stick with a true ivy-mark, and I believe some stick-makers actually train ivy to grow that way. One has to admire the skill and art of the carver, but such extremes I would regard as treatment likely to spoil the natural beauty of a good blackthorn stick.

There is a charisma about blackthorn walking sticks which has no need of the ornamentation designed to heighten the appeal of lesser woods. The rarity of these sticks, and their quality, both play a part, but there is something more. I have given away many sticks to friends, and later found that more are hanging up as wall decorations than are used for their intended purpose. I have been told, too, that a stick is destined to become a family heirloom. Others have sought me out to proudly show me blackthorn sticks which have been in their families for many years.

My first blackthorn was given to me over fifty years ago, by an Irish friend from Cork. It had a knob handle, and the thorns had been left on — a truly murderous weapon! In those days fashion dictated our wearing baggy plus-fours of shaggy tweed, and I well remember how the thorns became entangled in the cloth. Later the knob split at an old crack which had been glued together. One doesn't look a gift-horse in the mouth, but I'd always harboured a vague suspicion that was why I got the stick.

In spite of my Irish experience, I am convinced that the high regard for blackthorn emanates in some way from Ireland. More than once I have been asked, pointedly, if the stick I carried was an *Irish* blackthorn. Certainly Ireland has made blackthorn peculiarly its own, and an Irish exile will hang up a blackthorn stick decorated with a piece of green ribbon as a symbol of the Old Country. The officers of some Irish regiments carry blackthorn sticks, in contrast to the ash plants of their British counterparts. There is an obvious association, too, with the shillelagh, the blackthorn club. With the references in story and song we have nothing like that kind of tradition on this side of the Irish sea and my theory that it may have rubbed off on us seems not too implausible.

THE THEORY OF STRAIGHTENING SHANKS AND BENDING HANDLES

The actual methods I am going to describe in the next chapter were not evolved overnight, but are the final outcome of experiments over a considerable period and practical experience in solving specific problems. The methods work but I must warn that a certain amount of ingenuity and judgement is still required and it is not just like popping a bun into the oven and taking it out cooked.

Heating is the normal method of straightening and bending sticks, but my first trials proved that the traditional way by which ash and hazel can be successfully handled simply does not work for the more intractible blackthorn. I tapped the experience of several skilled practioners of orthodox stick-making and came away with the intelligence that, if a way of straightening blackthorn did exist, it was not common knowledge. However, one resort remained. If you want to learn anything about country-wise matters the place is the public bar of the local hostelry.

Accordingly, I took myself there one evening, when I knew it would be busy and after leading the conversation in the right direction, I put the vital question, how do you straighten blackthorn? After an unusually long silence one man said, "You can't straighten it, you've got to use stakes or splints and make it grow straight." Well, life is just too short for that process! Then, from a corner, came a second voice, "My grandfather used to tie his to the rafters of the cow byre and let them season." This was the clue I needed, and which opened the door.

Apart from the fact that I had no cows or byre, the method had other obvious limitations but it did indicate that blackthorn could be worked and the method was connected with the seasoning or drying process. Incidentally, it also confirmed that the old-timers could not have known of any quicker or more efficient method. My object now was to find a means of accelerating the process in the workshop.

Pondering over how to achieve that end, it struck me that the theoretical basis of the deformation of metals might apply equally to wood. Of course, other physical properties of the materials differ in the extreme, but the natural laws governing their behaviour, under heat and stress, are fundamentally similar and could be explained in the same terms. An understanding of the underlying theory always helps in finding a practical solution to any problem — the diagnosis before the cure.

For the technically-minded reader, therefore, the substance of the theory is contained in the following three definitions:

(i) Elastic limit — this is the highest stress (load) that can be applied to a material without producing permanent deformation.

(ii) Elastic deformation — this is produced by stress within the elastic range (i.e. under the elastic limit), in which the material will return to its original shape when the load is removed.

(iii) Permanent (or plastic) deformation — this occurs when the applied stress is greater than the elastic limit of the material. The material does not return to its original shape after removal of the load.

In the byre, the stick had been stressed by tying it to the rafter in a straightened position. At that time the wood was in the range of elastic deformation; after seasoning the stick had become *permanently* straightened, and for that to have happened, the wood must have been in the range of Permanent Deformation. Since the stress had not been altered during the entire operation, it has to be deduced that seasoning had lowered the elastic limit below the level of that stress, and had thus caused permanent deformation.

We know, that by reducing the elastic limit by seasoning (drying) to a level under the applied stress, we can achieve permanent deformation. Conversely, the applied stress could be raised above the elastic limit but that is limited to the amount required to straighten the stick. The above hypothesis appears to work in practice and is the basis of the methods I have used.

Here you might say, if seasoning is all that is required, one should be able to straighten any stick without heating, and you would be right – up to a point. I have indeed straightened blackthorn cold, and in one case took a pronounced bend out of a stick guaranteed to be over 50 years old. But this is feasible only with regular and gentle curves in relatively thin sticks – in heavier specimens with knuckles and acute changes of growth direction, quite savage deformation is needed, . Even more so in the bending of handles, higher temperatures and pressures are necessary.

The question arises, in the process of seasoning how far does the elastic limit fall? Certainly it never disappears completely, if it did the wood would have no elasticity and be brittle, which it is not. This retained elasticity appears to vary from wood to wood and even within the variations of Blackthorn. A stick containing heart wood is more difficult to work than one mainly comprising sapwood. That ash and hazel can be straightened by moderate heating suggests that their elastic limits are low. At the opposite extreme is yew, once used for longbows, in which the retained elastic limit must be high, in fact, approximating to the breaking strain as the bow will break before it distorts.

I have also experimented with beech, which proved to be more like blackthorn than did ash or hazel. All of my observations suggest strongly that each wood, after seasoning, has its own different level of innate retained elasticity, governing the readiness with which it can be manipulated. Blackthorn is in the upper range which could explain the difficulties I have described.

With the intracticable nature of blackthorn, heating is still indispensible. Its effect is to further lower the elastic limit and soften the tough fibres making the wood easier to work and reduce the risk of splitting.

It has been said that an ounce of practice is worth a ton of theory, and certainly one does not need to be a scientist to straighten a stick. None-the-less, an understanding of the principles involved does help in approaching a practical problem. To sum up, the elastic limit must be lowered by heating, to the extent required to bring the stick into the range of permanent deformation by the pressure available.

?
HE'LL NEVER STRAIGHTEN THAT ONE!

METHODS OF STRAIGHTENING AND BENDING

Before delving into the methods themselves, I need first to comment on the accompanying photographs illustrating "before and after" aspects of the techniques. A stick is a difficult subject to photograph, being all length and no thickness, and being notoriously difficult to capture full-length *and* in detail at the same time. Sticks in their natural condition have bends and twists in every direction, but cameras view in only one plane. Three dimensional or multi-exposure photography would be required to do justice to the subject – akin in many ways to a corkscrew. Imagine the confusion of someone who is asked to identify that cork-screw (which he has never seen before) from a photograph of the object taken "full-front" and at 90° to the axis. The photographs do not do justice to the complications of the original sticks!

The Fan-heater Method

You will recall from the previous chapter that the objective is simply to find a convenient method of holding a stick under pressure, while exposing it to a heat source sufficient to cause permanent deformation (i.e. straightening).

The provision of applied pressure was easy — two joiner's vices, at twenty five inch centres were mounted on my work-bench. The type is important, as the jaws are located on the side, and project only slightly above bench level — unlike an engineer's vice, the jaws of which sit on top of the bench. Two pieces of flat iron bar, 2½ inches by ½ inch by 3 feet long, dropped into the vices to rest on the guides made a powerful enough press. I have earlier mentioned the high pressures required, and note now that the resistance of some sticks actually deflected the flat bar by over half an inch. Incidentally, although these bars are termed iron by the trade, they are really low carbon steel.

Finding a suitable source of heat was more elusive to begin

with and a number of ideas were thought of and rejected, some of them, I might say, would have required the resources of an annealing shop. However, the old cow byre again supplied the simple train of thought and solution:— Cows, warm air, hot air, fan heater.

Completing the set-up, a five inch wide, length of insulating board was laid at a 45° angle behind the stick in order to divert the hot air downwards and along its length. Two shorter pieces in front formed a "tent", a kind of hot box with an aperture left for entry of the hot air. With a bent stick in the press, a three kilowatt fan heater was positioned in front of the aperture, flush with the bench top and about three inches from the stick.

The first test then was set to begin. Arbitrarily I gave it two hours heating, and left it to cool overnight. In the morning the stick came out — straight as a die! That first stick was a relatively easy one, with only a gentle curve to straighten, but it proved the theory, and what followed was only the overcoming of the practical problems in its application to more difficult specimens. The following are the main complications involved in the process:—

(i) With the heater positioned at the centre of the length of the stick, the area directly in front of the heater reaches a temperature of 180°C, but due to the distance the hot air has to travel and in its passage, giving up heat, the temperature near the ends may have fallen to 120° C. That is not high enough for a tough stick and during the heating cycle, the heater may have to be repositioned to heat the whole length of the stick equally.

(ii) When treating a stick with pronounced bends or twists, the full straightening pressure should not be applied until "operating" temperature is reached, otherwise the wood may be split.

(iii) As the process can handle only one plane at a time, and as most sticks have bends and twists in several planes, the stick must be turned and given two or more treatments.

(iv) Pressure should be applied progressively from one end only i.e. by the closing of one vice. As straightening proceeds, the overall length of the stick increases, and initial clamping of both ends will result in twisting in the middle.

(v) If the stick varies in thickness or has small radial bends, thin wooden wedges or distance pieces may have to be inserted to create pressure points.

(vi) It is impossible to recommend a specific heating time for any single operation, but it will generally lie between one and two hours. Second or third operations may take less time. A green stick will take longer, as the sap has to dry out. I prefer to use a partially seasoned stick, where nature has done some of the work for me!

Temperature is the key factor in working with blackthorn, and for straightening shanks 180°C, delivered by a 3 kw fan heater, is no more than adequate. For the purpose I would prefer to use a higher temperature to speed up the process in a variety of ways, but I have been unable to find a heater of this type, and of suitable design, with greater capacity. Having said that, all of the many stick shanks I have produced have been straightened by this method, and it continues to serve my purpose.

The bending of handles is quite another matter. The temperature achievable by the fan heater is too low and the heat not concentrated enough. While I did bend a few handles by this means, it was difficult and unsatisfactory. The fortuitous discovery of the hot air gun was a tremendous breakthrough, and provided the ideal solution.

The hot air gun method

The model of gun I use is rated at 1 kilo-watt capacity, and delivers air at 400°C through a 1¼ inch nozzle. As a measure of the intensity of this heat, metal turns red at just over 500°C and in operating the gun, the hot air flow must not be concentrated on one spot for too long. Alternatively the distance from nozzle to wood can be increased. The gun has no temperature adjustment but is quite easy to control. A slight charring is not inimical as the dark colour can blend in well with the appearance of the stick.

Unlike the fan heater, which can be set up and left for any desired time, the gun is a hand-held instrument. While it could be used for heating shanks in the press, this could be a laborious task. The higher temperature however is extremely useful for flattening knuckles and "obstreporous" bends.

I have, hitherto, not defined the term "knuckle" but it is self-explanatory really. It is a form of growth very common on branches, and looks exactly like the knuckle joint of a slightly bent middle finger. It generally cannot be removed completely, but can be modified to conform to the line of the shank and can make a not unattractive feature.

Forming handles is not a fool-proof operation, and entails considerable judgement. Very often one is working near to the limit of malleability of the wood. My early failure rate was quite high, and even experienced craftsmen would be content with 90% success. Variables include the nature of the wood (proportion of sap to heartwood, for example), the thickness of the handle, the degree of deformation required, and the shape of the handle.

Blackthorn strongly resists deformation on any large scale and the essence of success is to be able to decide how much a particular specimen will take without splitting. This is, no doubt, the reason for the scarcity of sticks with angled handles and the preponderance of knob handles. Except possibly in the case of thin and soft branches or shoots,

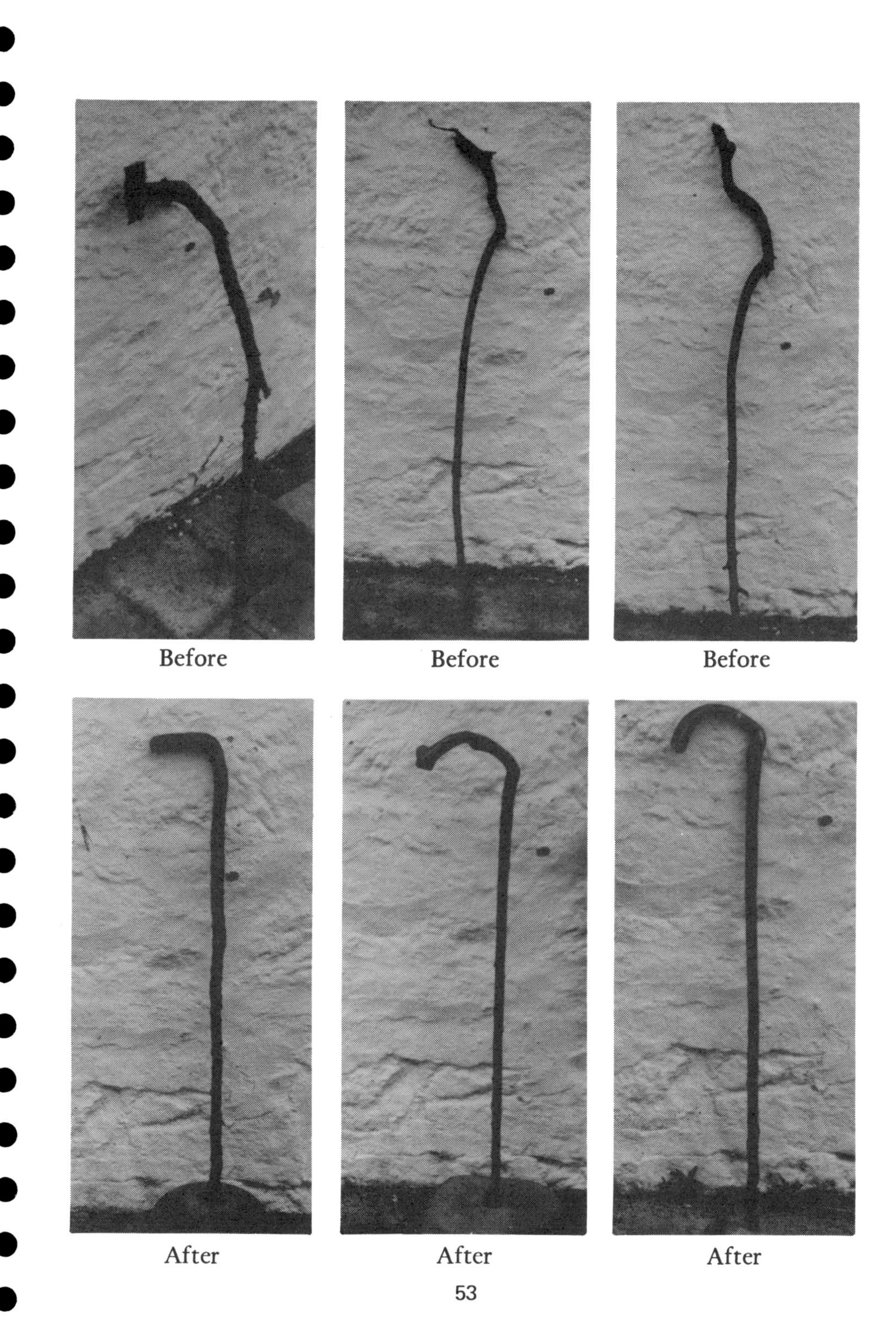

Before

Before

Before

After

After

After

blackthorn will not bend sufficiently to allow the fabrication of handles from a straight stick. A natural bend, or angle, however slight, must be present as a starting point. Where however, the angle is less than 90°C, forming an inverted "V" with the shank requiring to be opened up as opposed to bent down, either the wood splits in the corner or the top of the shank will bend back under the pressure. Either result makes the attempt a waste of time.

In sticks composed of a thin branch growing out of a thicker branch, intended for the handle, splitting inevitably occurs where the grain changes direction at the joint. A right angle can be formed by bending the top of the shank, but the result is an ugly handle. Unless the thick branch forms a natural right angle, or has enough wood in it to correct an irregular angle, I would leave it alone.

That leaves only two types on which I consider it is worth spending time and effort – the roots of shoots and the bends on branches. In each of these the essential property is that the grain follows the contour of shank and handle in an unbroken line. The treatment is the same for both. When cutting the branch or root, as much extra length as possible should be kept to provide the leverage for the bending force required. Otherwise a handle of short length will require to be extended by a piece of steel tube.

Now to the actual operation – a strong vice and a heavy bench, or at least one which is firmly secured, are essentials. The vice and bench have to act as a cantilever to a weight which can be in excess of 100 lbs.

The shank of the stick is held vertically in the vice with the handle in line with the edge of the bench. The embryo handle rests on a half round piece of wood which acts as a fulcrum at the point where bending is to begin.

A metal bucket is suspended by rope from the extension to the handle at a distance of up to eighteen inches from the fulcrum, depending on the amount of leverage

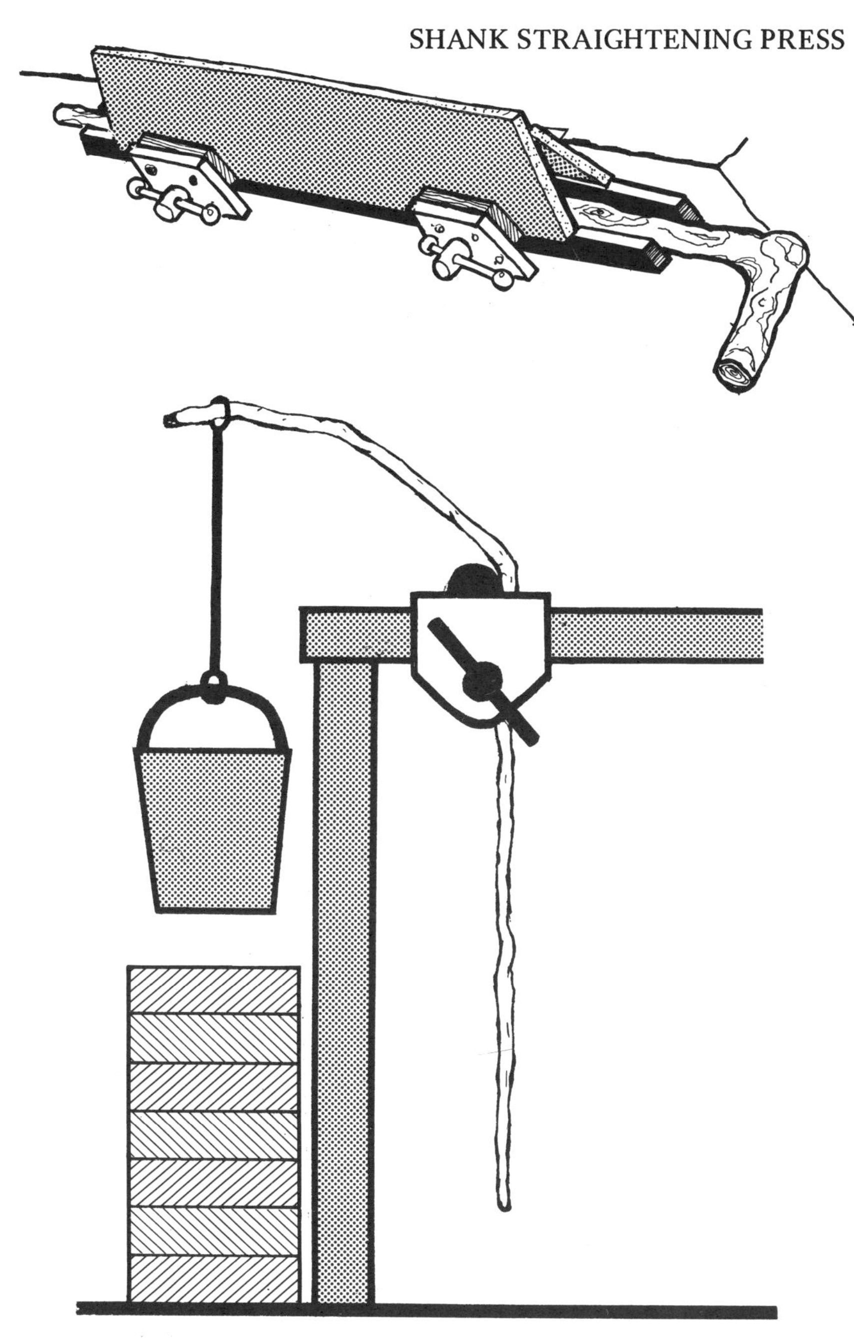

SHANK STRAIGHTENING PRESS

HANDLE BENDING SET-UP

estimated to be necessary. The bucket is then weighted with halfbricks, again to the estimated weight required. When completely filled the total weight is almost thirty-five pounds. There are two advantages in this method — the bucket can accommodate more weight in half bricks than whole ones, and the weight can be increased more gradually as the process goes on. It is advisable to stack layers of wood underneath the bucket, almost supporting it, to arrest its fall quickly if the handle shows signs of splitting. I use pieces of one inch plank, the topmost of which can be slid out as the bucket descends. Engineers will be able to calculate the bending force at this fulcrum — perhaps rather more than a hundred pounds.

Heating is begun by directing the nozzle of the gun at the end of the handle furthest from the fulcrum. As the wood softens and bending begins, the nozzle is moved progressively along the handle. Splitting, if it is going to occur, shows up first on the outer bark which is less elastic than the underlying wood fibres. Bark splits are not necessarily "fatal" as I have seen these open to almost ¼ inch before damage is caused to the fibres. However the signs must be watched carefully and the risks calculated. The weight of the bucket or the intensity of the heating may have to be adjusted. No two sticks are alike, and each has its own character and greater or lesser problems — some are easy, some are difficult, and some are downright impossible! It all boils down to experience and judgement.

In some cases the amount of bending required can be very considerable, depending on the original angle and the final handle shape intended. As a rule the thickness and nature of the wood dictates how much bending the handle will stand. As the handle bends, the bucket descends, and it is not unknown for it to finish resting on the floor. having descended through an arc of over two feet.

In both processes, straightening shanks and bending handles, some damage may be caused to the surface of the wood and occasionally it may buckle or split. If the split is longitudinal, running in the same direction as the wood fibres, it is not harmful, but a transverse split across the fibres, if deep enough, may mean the scrapping of the stick. The criterion is that the strength of the stick must not be adversely affected. Cosmetically, although a damaged surface need not be unsightly, I see no objection to the use of a natural coloured plastic wood filler which will be homogeneous with the wood if properly keyed in.

An essential fitment for a stick is the ferrule, without which the stick would not last very long. There are two types – brass and rubber. The brass ferrule has to be fitted and pinned to the shank, and is more difficult to replace when worn. The rubber ferrule is really a push-on cap, and simple to replace; it further has a non-slip surface. Both types can be bought in various inside diameters.

The Jack and Jig Method

This, the third and last method, might properly be called an afterthought and originated in my regard for my own creature comfort. My workshop is large and can be cold and draughty, and is, moreover, outside the house. In contrast my study is cosy and small enough to be heated by an electric radiator. Forced indoors, this is where I spend most of my time, and leaving it for the workshop on a cold night can be a disagreeable prospect.

Rejecting the idea of bringing the bench and vice set-up into my study, which could have proved a most unpopular move, I began looking for a way of using my study radiator beyond mere personal comfort. My answer was the jack and jig method. The jig (I can't think of a better term) is just a hardwood frame of two uprights strongly secured to a wood base and reinforced with a crosspiece. Each upright measures fourteen inches long by four inches wide by one inch thick, and is slotted to two inches from the top. I made three such frames, respectively five inches, six inches and twelve inches between the uprights for different uses.

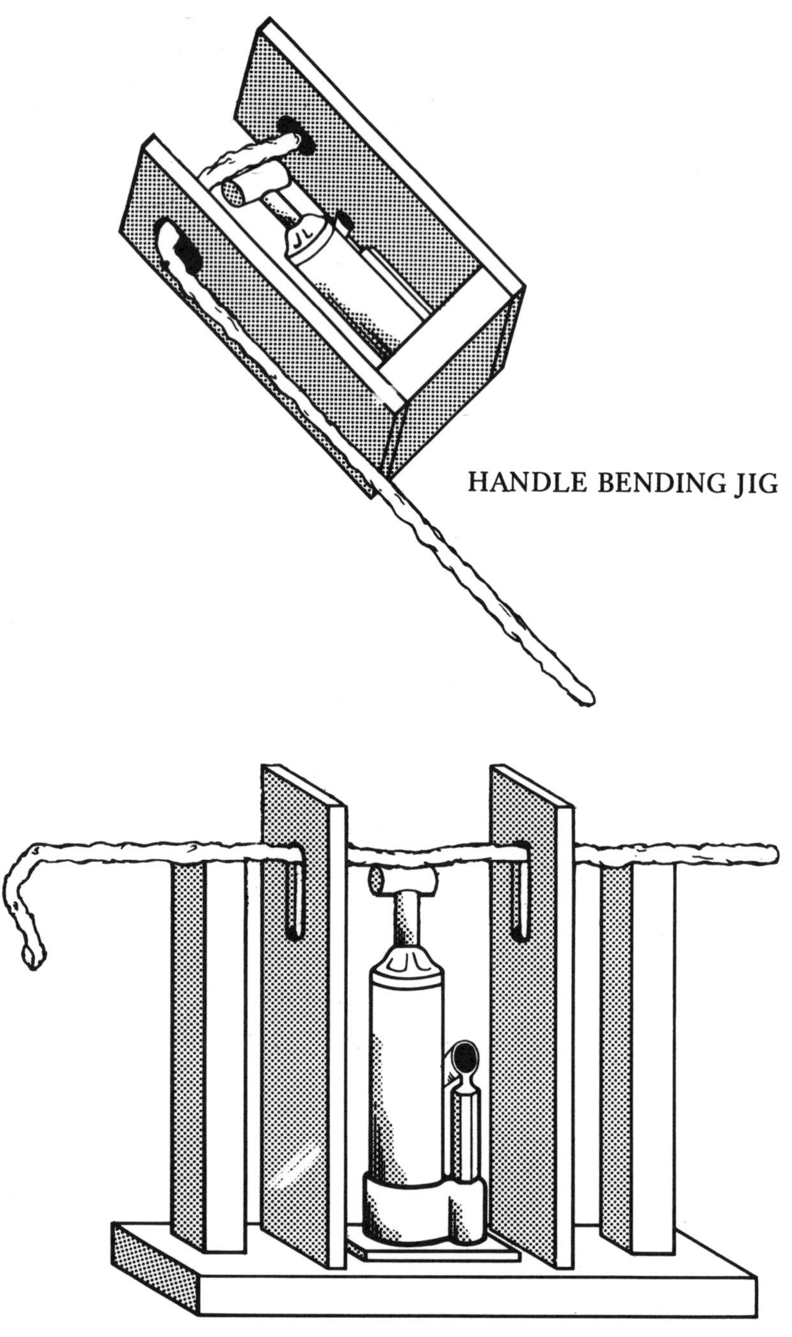

HANDLE BENDING JIG

SHANK STRAIGHTENING JIG

The jack is a two ton capacity motorist's hydraulic jack. Lest anyone be smiling indulgently at the thought of using a two ton jack to bend a stick, let me point out that with a short length in the narrow frame, I have to use the extension handle to gain enough purchase. The end of the piston is fitted with a round piece of wood on which the stick rests.

For straightening, the stick is placed in the slots with the curve downwards, and pressed upwards by the jack which sits on the base board. As the curve straightens the ends tend to dip, and it is necessary to insert wooden supports between the stick and the extension to the base to keep the stick straight.

For bending handles the same procedure applies, with the handle in the slots and the shank in line with the side of the upright. It is advisable to wrap the handle in aluminium foil where it comes in contact with the edge of the slots. The sliding action as the handle straightens or bends can abraid the surface of the bark. The foil to use is not the paper thin type, but the kind for pie dishes and the like.

When the set-up is taut and firm, with the stick held in position by the jack, the frame is lifted and laid on its side with the top on or near the guard of the electric radiator. I have been unable to measure the temperature achievable in the stick, but estimate it to be about 300°C from a 1 kw bar, and thus superior to the fan heater. As heating goes on, the wood softens and the piston of the jack is raised gradually until the desired shape of shank or handle is reached. The stick must be allowed to cool to room temperature before removal from the frame.

Before you begin to imagine that this technique renders the other two redundant, it is an adjunct to them rather than a substitute. It is useful for straightening easy curves, and has the advantage of being able to stretch the wood fibres by forcing the curve to reverse above its axis. It is particularly good for cold-straightening finished sticks which have warped as does occasionally happen. It cannot however, flatten knuckles or angular or small-radius bends, the kind of problem most frequently met on branches. Similarly with handles its range of application is limited — if the angle is significantly more than 90°, for example; and there is in any case little control over the finished shape. In many cases a certain amount of preliminary work can be done, especially in straightening operations, which will ease the task of finishing in the press. The technique should be seen as an extra weapon in the armoury, and a welcome addition when one remembers that it can be employed, literally, while in one's armchair spending no extra on fuel. I wonder how many great discoveries have been made by physically lazy men with active minds?

I would counsel the beginner, "Try your prentice hand in this fashion, especially on shoots." The apparatus is easy to set up and not at all costly. If you can select shoots with root or knob handles, you will achieve blackthorn walking sticks of reasonable quality. The other two methods are necessary for the production of sticks of higher quality, but they do require investment in expensive equipment, especially if this has to be bought new. For the newcomer, these methods also demand a level of dedication and a degree of ingenuity which might prove defeating.

THE LAST EXPERIMENT

The narrative, to this point, reads like an uninterrupted success story. As an addendum, and to balance that impression, I now reveal an essay which proved not an unqualified triumph. I had toyed with the idea from time to time, and had been struck by the sheer simplicity of its solution to the problems of straightening. My acquisition of the hot air gun, with its offer of localised and concentrated heat, made a practical trial possible.

Simply expressed, the idea involved stretching the stick longtitudinally under exposure to heat. "Stretching" is perhaps too powerful – pulling until the bends straightened is more accurate. An understanding of the mechanics involved is necessary. I have already emphasised the importance (and extent) of leverage forces in dealing with handles; in this process of pulling, the leverage is that supplied by the bend itself. For example, a bend with a three inch radius from the central axis of the stick has the equivalent power of a three inch lever; a one inch radius bend, has only one inch leverage. It follows that, as a bend straightens, the leverage reduces, and disappears as the stick becomes straight. The effects of these dimensions are insignificant compared with the eighteen inch lever required for bending handles, and it follows that the force must be largely applied by direct loading.

This approach is undeniably logical, and theoretically sound – but could the required direct force be successfully applied in practice? I employed the following method. One end of the stick was attached by rope to a work shop rafter, and the other end to a loaded bucket weighing around 60 lbs. Three tests were carried out on sticks of varying thickness and degree of disfigurement. In each case the bend was heated by the gun for thirty minutes at 400°C. The radius of the bend was measured before and after heating, to determine whether any success had been achieved.

Results	Diameter of Stick	Radius of Bond before Treatment	Radius of Bond after Treatment
Test 1	1⅛″	4″	3″
Test 2	1″	1½″	1½″
Test 3	¾″	1″	¼″

In test 1, the leverage of the considerable bend, even in a thicker stick, was responsible for partial straightening, but soon that diminishing leverage was overcome by the resistance of the wood. In test 2, the initial leverage was insufficient even to begin the process of straightening against the resistance of a fairly thick piece of wood. Test 3 was most nearly successful – the stick was at the low end of the range of acceptable thickness for a walking stick, and offered least resistance to the weight, but even here the leverage supplied by the small radius of bend faded before complete straightening was achieved.

The theory was proved, but the practical obstacle of finding a way to apply sufficient force remains unsolved. My somewhat "Heath Robinson" arrangement had reached its practical limit – increasing the load would meet severe difficulties. Someone of a mechanical bent might take up where I left off, designing a kind of rack using a steel frame equipped with lever and ratchet arrangement to operate a roller winch. For me, the older methods are tried, tested and will remain adequate. A pity – it might all have been so simple!

Readers might wonder why I have devoted a chapter to what proved, after all, to be an abortive experiment. Apart from an interest in the mechanics and the results of a novel approach, the exercise confirmed the vital importance of leverage, screw vices and hydraulic ram used in the other methods. I would go further and say that, notwithstanding my experience of these other methods, I did not anticipate and was surprised by the degree of resistance to deformation offered by blackthorn even under exposure to extreme heat. It is impossible to estimate the ultimate force which would be required in the direct loading method, but I would guess it to be nearer 200 lbs than 100 lbs.

OBJET TROUVÉ

Although somewhat outside the scope of my defined subject matter, there is another facet of blackthorn which I consider worthy of mention. If I were asked to sketch, or represent in some other way, the outline of a tree which would be typical of the species, I would find the task impossible. Without the leaf, the vast variety of forms might be difficult to recognise as members of a family. Its highly irregular branching habit creates a range of shapes which, without exaggerating, might be likened to free form sculpture.

The French, have a name for it — *objet trouve,* a distinctive type of *objet d'art.* Literally, it means a found object as opposed to something manufactured. The group includes any natural object with artistic possibilities, such as abstract sculptures created from weathered tree-stumps and drift-wood, mineral rocks and other materials, and in which, natural conformation and colour qualify eccentric blackthorn growths to be included. Such blackthorn pieces could find application in the creation of centrepieces for flower arrangements.

Closely related to this artistic concept is the adaptation of a natural object for a practical purpose, while still retaining the aesthetically pleasing natural form. This is the essence of the attraction of making blackthorn walking sticks. While searching for branches suitable for walking sticks a great deal of ground has to be covered. A hedge several hundred yards long might yield nothing, while a clump of only two or three bushes might produce as many good specimens, gold is where you find it. In such exhaustive searches you inevitably will come across the bonus of an unusual growth of a shape which the imagination can turn into an original and highly individual article. In this way I have created a number of pipe racks, and I feel it worthwhile to describe the method used.

The specification is simple — a firm base from which emerges a more or less horizontal arm, into which holes can be drilled for receiving the pipes. The only vital measurement is the

OBJET TROUVÉ

Blackthorn branches as cut

Examples of Pipe Racks

diameter of these holes — they must be ¾ inch minimum — and therefore, the arm should have a thickness of at least 1¼ inch to provide the required strength. There are two basic types of piperack. The first consists of a thicker branch which, with the bottom sawn off to a flat, forms the base, and a thinner branch rising from it and growing parallel; parallel shape can be induced by vice and heater. In the second type there are two branches of similar diameter, growing nearly parallel to each other, but curved or twisted. One branch can then provide the base, and stability comes from the curve or twist. In both types the holes should be drilled at 1½ inch centres, and at angles which will allow clearance for the pipe stems. Before varnishing, careful and selective filing and sandpapering are used to bring out the rich living glow of the wood.

Some readers may be attracted to blackthorn without wishing to become involved in manufacturing walking sticks and in the complications of that art. Those with artistic leanings might find the above suggestions allow involvement with the magic of blackthorn in a compelling and rewarding way.

SNAP!
OOOH!

CULZEAN BAY

In the account of where blackthorn may be found, I did not identify the locations where different varieties can be seen. To have done so would not have served much purpose as they are widely scattered, often not easy to find or difficult of access. It would be an unfair omission, however, if I made no attempt to show the way to any reader interested enough to go out and actually see what I have described.

One area which contains examples of most of the variations, with the exception of larger trees which are scarce anywhere, is that centred on the coast-line of Culzean Bay. A prime attraction for many visitors will be the accessability of all the sites by car on roads open to the public and with convenient car-parks. The need for walking, is minimal and in some cases it is not even necessary to leave the car.

An added reward could be that, after passing spectacular views of the coast and through fine wooded country, the journey ends at Culzean Country Park acknowledged to be the "Most magnificent country park in Britain" and Culzean Castle, one of the star properties of the National Trust for Scotland. While I think many people would prefer to spend more time, the tour and return could be accomplished in an afternoon from the starting point – the town of Ayr to the north.

I have used Culzean Bay as a reference, see sheet No. 70, Ordnance Survey, but the area involved extends slightly north, taking in the fishing village of Dunure and south, beyond Culzean to Maidenhead Bay. It is my purpose to point to the locations where blackthorn is found but not to describe it in any detail.

Setting out from Ayr, take the A719 for about seven miles to the Dunure turn-off. The first blackthorn is seen on the steep wooded left bank of the road going into the village. Straight on through the village to the outskirts, the entrance to the public car-park is on the right. From that a short walk takes one to a vantage point from which can be seen a jumbled mass of low peaks and ravines, studded here and there with blackthorn. To the left, in the middle distance are thickets growing on the higher slopes.

Continuing the journey, turn right when leaving the car-park, taking the southern exit from the village to rejoin the A719. On the way, there is a blackthorn hedge on the left and more on the old, disused, Ayr to Turnberry railway line over which the road passes.

Turning right again on to the A719, the next stop will be Croy Bay. Before that, however, is the Electric Brae, a stopping place for thousands of visitors. Here, apparently, the law of gravity is flouted and cars free-wheel up hill and have to be powered down-hill.

Croy Bay is reached by taking the turn-off to the right, which is well sign-posted. The road runs down to a public car-park and then continues to the beach, a few hundred yards further on. The area, north and south of the road, is, literally, thick with blackthorn on the crags and in the steep glen.

Leaving Croy Bay turn right again on the A719 which now runs to meet the B7023 at a junction facing Mochrum Hill, the highest point in the district. Turn right and you are now only a couple of miles from the entrance to Culzean.

The blackthorn at Culzean is not extensive or unusual, in itself, the interest lies in its location and function. It grows on sand dunes down to the high tide mark and has been dwarfed by the winds and salt spray, reaching a height of only two or three feet. Its value is its usefulness as a barrier against dune erosion which is a problem at parts of the coast. It could have been planted for that purpose, but more likely it originated from a near-by roadside hedge and thicket.

Visitors reaching Culzean might well opt to seek refreshment in the Park restaurant but, for the indefatigable who wish to see the last blackthorn, the following is the way. From a

DUNURE

Dunure Castle
with blackthorn
in fore-ground

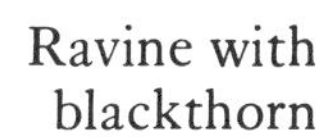

Ravine with
blackthorn

Blackthorn
on crags

CROY BAY

View from public car park

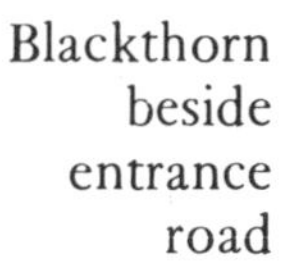

Blackthorn beside entrance road

View from shore of blackthorn on slopes and crags

CULZEAN

Culzean Castle

Culzean Bay from battlements of castle

Blackthorn on crags

Culzean Bay
from north.
As seen from
A719

Blackthorn
on dunes:
down to high
tide mark.
Note flotsam

Hedge and
thicket on
road presumed
origin of
thickets on
dunes

starting point of the car-park, in front of the Castle, the vehicle road to the south leads ultimately to the Park boundary. There, a stile gives access to a short road leading to the beach. On the right of this road is the blackthorn hedge, mentioned above, with an attendant thicket. The dunes lie a short distance to the right along the beach.

I don't know how many people will want or be able to follow this route but I can think of no better way of spending a summer day.

The two castles shown are of considerable historical interest, illustrating the rise of the Kennedy family over a period of 500 years.

Dunure Castle, 1300 A.D. or earlier, was where Gilbert Kennedy roasted the Commendator of Crossraguel Abbey to force him to sign over the Abbey lands.

Culzean Castle built late in the 18th century by the same family as a great Baronial house was gifted in 1945 by the 5th Marquis of Ailsa to the National Trust.

ORIGINS OF FOLK-LORE AND SUPERSTITION

Many trees have folk-lore and superstition associated with them. Early man believed that trees were the abode of spirits, either good or bad, and attributed to them, magical powers. Generally, the superstitions were irrational with no rhyme or reason for their being. In that respect, however, I think those of blackthorn are the exception and plausible reasons can be adduced for their origins.

In its folk-lore, it has given to the language the term "blackthorn winter", universally used as a synonym, a convenient code name, for a late frost which strikes at the time of blackthorn blossom and stops the fruit setting.

Blackthorn Winter

To a predominantly agricultural people, the onset of such a frost, hard enough to kill tree blossom, would have been a considerable seasonal set-back. In that context, the designation "blackthorn", to mark the time when the frost occurs, is logical, the appellation "winter", however, I find difficult to understand.

Blackthorn blossoms in late March or early April, according to latitude and climate and is thus a spring flowering plant. Perhaps being of a literal mind, I would have assumed the correct name to be blackthorn"spring".

The commonly held explanation for this, to me, apparent anomaly is metaphorical, by definition, the description of something as being that which it only resembles. To paraphrase, a hard frost in March might be called "winter in spring".

There are seeming analogies in the use of summer to describe spells of fine weather late in the year when seasonal summer is past – St. Luke's summer, 18th October, All Hallows' summer, 18th October; St. Martin's summer, 11th November (Martinmas); Indian summer, anytime in Autumn.

For these, I would not dispute the usual explanation but I feel vaguely dissatisfied in its application to "blackthorn winter". Three of the above are connected with saints and the fourth, Indian summer is an American importation with a slightly different implication. Blackthorn winter seems to be the "odd man out". I have looked for a literal explanation and offer the following. While any conclusions cannot be proved, I hope the reasoning and evidence will still be of interest in themselves.

I am concerned with origins and seek to show that in the beginning, blackthorn winter, literally, could have meant what it said. To do so, it is necessary to demonstrate that blackthorn could have blossomed in what was regarded as a seasonal winter month. The first step requires a definition of spring.

Astronomically, that begins at the Spring Equinox when the sun crosses the equator and days and nights are of equal length, in our calendar, the 21st of March. This has only limited reference to growing conditions; according to the seasonal divisions of the calendar, spring begins on the 1st of March.

The act of Pope Gregory XIII changed the then, calendar in relation to the solar year and in the same degree to climate. The change is important in determining the historical time of flowering of blackthorn.

The Gregorian Calendar

The Julian calendar introduced by Julius Caesar in 46 B.C. was in use until 1582. It contained, however, a small plus error in the length of its year which had caused it to fall behind the solar year.

In 1582, Gregory corrected the discrepancy by changing the 5th to the 15th of October, thus eliminating eleven calendar days. The leap year was adjusted to prevent continuing slippage and constitutes the basis of our modern calendar.

Catholic countries adopted the change immediately but Protestant countries not until much later; England and Scotland in 1752 and Russia not until 1918.

The change in the calendar was not understood by the people who thought they were losing eleven days out of their lives. Their cry was "Give us back our eleven days". Another cause of distress was that their Saints' days had been changed. A case in point; under the old calendar, the flowering of Hawthorn or May coincided with May day.

By the new style calendar, hawthorn flowers later and the "magic" May blossom was no longer available for the rituals and ceremonies of the Maypole and Morris dancing. (I believe that, today, forcing in greenhouses is being considered to have the May blossom ready for the 1st May).

A consequence of the change was to put back the date of the Spring Equinox from the 11th March in the Julian calendar to the 21st March in the New Style, as it came to be called.

More important, for this research, the calendar date of the beginning of spring was delayed in effect (although not actually) until the 11th March.

This means that the seasonal conditions of what was the 18th February in the Julian calendar are the same as those of 1st March in our calendar. Putting it in a simpler way; February was a warmer month than it is now.

For the purpose of the argument, the historical date of the blossoming of blackthorn has been brought closer to calendar winter. Is there any other factor which could push it over the border?

Mini Ice-ages

The name and conception of blackthorn winter is certainly very old and must have existed throughout the alternating cold and warm spells of past centuries, as exemplified by various mini ice-ages.

In a universally warm period, growth would have been earlier and blackthorn could have blossomed in what were winter months, according to the calendar. If the name blackthorn winter had been coined during an extensive warm period, is it not just possible that the name literally meant what it said?

An advantage about speculating on the far past is that no-one can refute you.

Ice or Frost Saints.

The name was given to four early Christian saints whose days fall in the second week of May -- St. Mamertus, 11th; St. Pancras, 12th, St. Servatius, 13th and St. Boniface, 14th.

I have included them in this chapter solely because references state, categorically, that they are so called because their dates fall in the period of blackthorn winter. There is even debate as to what is the exact period whether the 11th, 12th, 13th or the 12th, 13th and 14th.

Why should the name be given to those four saints when the days of others fall in colder times of the year and when did blackthorn bloom in May?

These are questions which I must leave unanswered. Blackthorn appears to extend its mysteries into its folk-lore.

Peewits' Pinch

Again, I include this because the term is described as the same as blackthorn winter, occurring in March when peewits begin nesting on the ground and so feel the "pinch".

Compare this with the last heading and the mystery deepens.

The Unlucky Tree

Blackthorn was regarded as an unlucky tree but in its case, plausible reasons for its reputation can be advanced. From Roman times, and they borrowed it from the ancient Egyptians, black has been the colour of mourning. The Romans marked the unlucky days on their calendars with charcoal, hence black letter day.

It has come into the language as a word symbolic of death and evil in conceptions like Black Art with the devil portrayed in black and names as Black Friday, Black Cap, Black Death, Black Book and a couple of dozen more, all in the same vein.

With the connotation of the colour and evil it would be an easy and natural step if illogical to dignify the adjective and label blackthorn unlucky, just because it is black in name and colour.

A more prosaic but perhaps supportive explanation is that blackthorn can be dangerous as my own experience, after being punctured by a thorn, demonstrates. The unlucky belief may have begun as a simple admonition, possibly by mothers to children, to keep away from it. Certainly anyone falling into a blackthorn bush, indeed, would have been unlucky.

Crown of Thorns

In the Christian era the prejudice would have been strengthened by the belief that Christ's crown of thorns was blackthorn. That is classed as legend but could be true. Blackthorn is found in the Middle East and it would conform to the brutal logic and purpose of the Romans to use the most vicious thorn available. If the legend is based on fact, then simply to see the thorns brings home the savagery of the deed beyond the power of description.

In some parts of England the belief led to two superstitious customs. One was a fertility rite. Early on New Years' morning a crown made of blackthorn was calcined in an oven and the ashes scattered on the fields.

My interpretation of the reason behind the tradition is that it was a symbolic act of revenge against the blackthorn which had lent itself to the crown of thorms. The participants solicited divine approval and expected a reward. The scattering of the ashes on the fields indicated that they would prefer the reward to be in the form of better crops.

In the other, blackthorn was scorched in the fire and then hung among the mistletoe at Christmas for good luck. The reasoning would be the same but in this case the doers apparently left it to divine discretion as to the shape the luck should take.

POSTSCRIPT

When I began, nearly three years ago, with the modest ambition of finding a way of making a Blackthorn walking stick for myself, I had no idea how deeply I was going to become involved. It has been said that my hobby is making walking sticks. In fact, although I value them, they are only the by-products of the more compelling pursuit of search and discovery, the process and results of which I have tried to portray.

I came to realise that Blackthorn is a unique plant with strange and complicated growth, too cursorily glossed over in the books I have read. That being so, this book may go some way towards filling the gap. At the least it might encourage country walkers to look at Blackthorn with a new eye and greater interest.

Making Blackthorn walking sticks is a craft and if I have advanced the technique, it is right that the knowledge should be shared. There is no lasting satisfaction in churning out walking sticks in a secret workshop. Having accomplished what I set out to do, my own interest has waned and is confined now to looking for unusual and rare growths.

There is a great and growing interest in country crafts, and I hope to have opened a door to a revitalisation of one of the oldest of them all.